KU-659-910

People who know no German at all.

People who know some German already.

People who studied German at school.

People who didn't study German at school.

People who didn't like how languages were taught at school.

People who are amazed by just how closely grammar books resemble furniture assembly instructions.

Who is this book for?

People who think they can't learn a foreign language.

People who've listened to one of Paul Noble's audio courses.

People who haven't listened to one of Paul Noble's audio courses.

People learning German for the first time.

People coming back to the language after a break.

People curious about whether they can learn a language.

People who feel confused by the way languages are normally taught.

Contents

Did you know you
already speak German?

Did you know you already speak German?

Did you know you already speak German? That you speak it every day? That you read and write it every day? That you use it with your friends, with your family, at work, down the post office – even in the shower when you read the label on the shampoo bottle?

Were you aware of that fact?

Well, even if you weren't, it's nevertheless true.

Of course, you might not have realised at the time that what you were reading / saying / writing was actually German but I can prove to you that it was. Just take a look at these words below:

Winter	Name	Warm	Baby	
Land	Blind	Wild	Arm	Hand
Finger	Blond	Hammer	Horn	

Ring	Wind	Butter	Bitter
Sand	Wolf	Hunger	Rose
Nest	Gold		

Have you read through them?
yes? Good.

Now, answer me this, are they:

A: English words
B: German words
C: Both

Well, if you're reading this book then you're clearly already a highly intelligent person with good judgement, so you will have correctly chosen "C".

Yes, these are words that we have in English *but* they also exist in German, having originally come into English from Germanic languages. And these are by no means isolated examples of words that exist in both German and English but rather they are merely the tip of a *truly enormous* iceberg.

In fact, around half of all English words have close equivalents in German. Yes, that's right, *half!*

If we begin using these words, together with an extremely subtle method that shows you how to put them into sentences in a way that's almost effortless, then becoming a competent German speaker becomes really quite easy.

The only thing that *you* will need to do to make this happen is to follow the three simple rules printed on the following pages. These rules will explain to you how to use this book so that you can begin unlocking the German language for yourself in a matter of hours.

Well, what are you waiting for? Turn the page!

Rule Number 1:

Don't skip anything!

Using this book is extremely simple – and highly effective – *if* you follow its three simple rules.

If you don't want to follow them then I recommend that, instead of reading the book, you use it to prop up a wobbly coffee table, as it won't work if you don't follow the rules. Now get ready – because here's the first one!

Each and every little thing in this book has been put where it is, in a very particular order, for a very particular reason. So, if the book asks you to read or do something, then do it! Who's the teacher after all, you or me, eh?

Also, each part of the book builds on and reinforces what came before it. So, if you start skipping sections, you will end up confused and lost! Instead, you should just take your time and gently work your way through the book at your own pace – *but without skipping anything*!

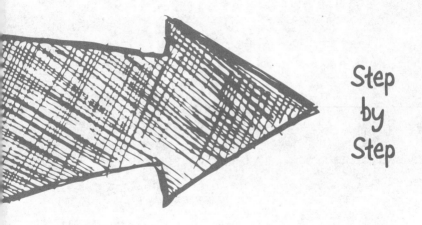

Step
by
Step

Rule Number 2:

Don't try to memorise anything!

Trying to jam things into your head is boring *and* it doesn't work. People often cram for tests and then forget everything the moment they walk out of the exam. Clearly, we don't want that happening here.

Instead, I have designed this book so that any word or idea taught in it will come up multiple times. You don't need to worry about trying to remember or memorise anything because the necessary repetition is actually already built in. In fact, trying to memorise what you're learning is likely to hinder rather than help your progress.

So, just work your way through the book in a relaxed way and, if you happen to forget something, don't worry because, as I say, you will be reminded of it again, multiple times, later on.

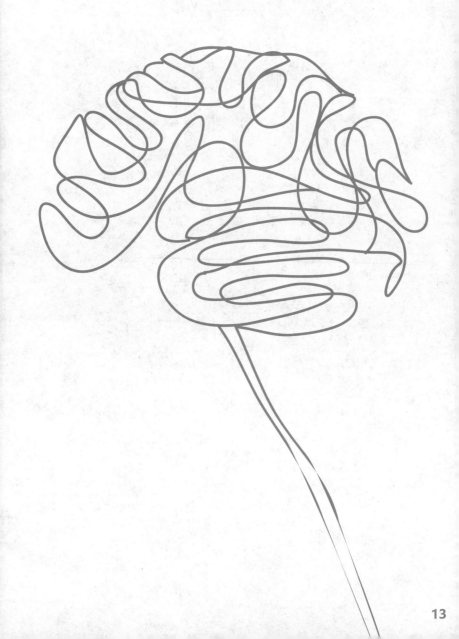

Rule Number 3:
Cover up!

No, I'm not being a puritan grandmother and telling you to put on a long-sleeved cardigan. Instead, I'm asking you to take a bookmark or piece of paper and use it to cover up any **red text** that you come across as you work your way through the book.

These **red bits** are the answers to the various riddles, challenges and questions that I will pose as I lead you into the German language. If you read these answers without at least trying to work out the solutions to the various riddles and challenges first, then the book simply won't work for you.

So make sure to use something to cover up the bits of **red text** in the book while you have a go at trying to work out the answers. It doesn't matter if you sometimes get them wrong because it is by trying to think out the answers that you will learn how to use the language.

Trust me on this, you will see that it works from the very next page of this book.

Take a look at the page on the right to see how to use your bookmark or piece of paper to cover up correctly.

And "I saw the father"?

Ich habe den Vater gesehen.
(ikh hah-ber dain far-ter ge-zay-urn)

Again, notice that, since "the father" is masculine and is having something done to him (in this case he is being seen), the "der" has become "den".

Let's practise the same change again with "the film". What is "the film" in German?

der Film
(dair film)

And so how would you say "I have seen the film"?

Ich habe den Film gesehen.
(ikh hah-ber dain film ge-zay-urn)

How about "I saw the film"?

Ich habe den Film gesehen.
(ikh hah-ber dain film ge-zay-urn)

And "I did see the film"?

Ich habe den Film gesehen.
(ikh hah-ber dain film ge-zay-urn)

"I have bought", "I bought" and "I did buy" in German are all:

Ich habe gekauft.
(ikh hah-ber ge-kowft)

So how would you say "I bought the milk"?

Ich habe die Milch gekauft.
(ikh hah-ber dee milkh ge-kowft)

And what about "I bought the beer"?

Ich habe das Bier gekauft.
(ikh hah-ber das bee-er ge-kowft)

Finally, "I bought the tea"?

Ich habe den Tee gekauft.
(ikh hah-ber dain tay ge-kowft)

"The ticket" in German is:

die Eintrittskarte
(dee ine-trits-kart-er)

This literally means "the entry card".

So how would you say "I have bought the ticket", "I bought the ticket", "I did buy the ticket"?

Ich habe die Eintrittskarte gekauft.

Make sure to cover up any red words, just like this!

see the film"?

Ich habe den Film gesehen.
(ikh hah-ber dain film ge-zay-urn)

And so how would you say "I haven't seen the film", "I didn't see the film" (literally "I have the film not seen")?

Ich habe den Film nicht gesehen.
(ikh hah-ber dain film nikht ge-zay-urn)

And "I saw the father"?

Ich habe den Vater gesehen.
(ikh hah-ber dain far-ter ge-zay-urn)

Again, notice that, since "the father" is masculine and is having something done to him (in this case he is being seen), the "der" has become "den".

Let's practise the same change again with "the film". What is "the film" in German?

der Film
(dair film)

And so how would you say "I have seen the film"?

Ich habe den Film gesehen.
(ikh hah-ber dain film ge-zay-urn)

How about "I saw the film"?

Ich habe den Film gesehen.
(ikh hah-ber dain film ge-zay-urn)

And "I did see the film"?

Ich habe den Film gesehen.
(ikh hah-ber dain film ge-zay-urn)

"I have bought", "I bought" and "I did buy" in German are all:

Ich habe gekauft.
(ikh hah-ber ge-kowft)

So how would you say "I bought the milk"?

Ich habe die Milch gekauft.
(ikh hah-ber dee milkh ge-kowft)

And what about "I bought the beer"?

Ich habe das Bier gekauft.
(ikh hah-ber das bee-er ge-kowft)

Finally, "I bought the tea"?

Ich habe den Tee gekauft.
(ikh hah-ber dain tay ge-kowft)

"The ticket" in German is:

die Eintrittskarte
(dee ine-trits-kart-er)

This literally means "the entry card".

So how would you say "I have bought the ticket", "I bought the ticket", "I did buy the ticket"?

Ich habe die Eintrittskarte gekauft.
(ikh hah-ber dee ine-trits-kart-er ge-kowft)

Then, having tried to work out the answer, uncover and check!

Ich habe den Film gesehen.
(ikh hah-ber dain film ge-zay-urn)

And so how would you say "I haven't seen the film", "I didn't see the film" (literally "I have the film not seen")?

Ich habe den Film nicht gesehen.
(ikh hah-ber dain film nikht ge-zay-urn)

CHAPTER 1

Can you come over tonight?

"Can you come over tonight?"
Not such a complicated sentence in English really, is it?
Or is it…?

I have taught many people over the years, ranging from those who know no German at all through to those who may have studied German for several years at school, and yet whether they have studied the language before or not, many of them still struggle to construct a basic sentence like this when I first meet them.

Admittedly, they might know how to say other far less useful things, like "I'm 37 years old and have two sisters and a goldfish" – an unusual conversation opener from my perspective – but they nevertheless can't ask someone to come over later.

Well, in just a few minutes' time, you *will* be able to do this – even if you've never learnt any German before.

Just remember though: ***don't* skip anything, *don't* waste your time trying to memorise anything but *do* use your bookmark to cover up anything red you find on each page.**

Okay now, let's begin!

"I can" in German is:

Ich kann
(pronounced "ikh kan"[1])

And the word for "begin" in German is:

beginnen
(pronounced "baig-in-urn")

---

1   Under each set of German words, you'll find pronunciation guidance. If there's something that's particularly tricky to pronounce, however, I'll also add a little footnote like this one to give you some extra help. I'm going to do this now in fact, to help you with the "**ch**" at the end of "i**ch**". The "**ch**" on the end of "i**ch**" is pronounced in a similar way to the letter "**h**" at the beginning of the English words "**h**uge" and "**h**uman". Try saying "**h**uge" and then take the "uge" bit away. The kind of hissing "**h**" sound that you are left with is what the "**ch**" in "i**ch**" should sound like; I've written it in the pronunciation guidance as a kind of "ikh" sound. With a bit of practice, you'll get the hang of it!

So how would you say "I can begin"?

Ich kann beginnen
(ikh kan baig-in-urn)

Did you remember to cover up the red words while you worked out the answer?

"Not" in German is:

nicht
(nikht)

Now again, what is "I can"?

ich kann
(ikh kan)

So how would you say "I can not"?

ich kann nicht
(ikh kan nikht)

And so how would you say "I cannot begin"?

Ich kann nicht beginnen.
(ikh kan nikht baig-in-urn)

The word for "bring" in German is:

bringen
(bring-urn)

You will notice very quickly that the word for "bring" in German – "bringen" – is very similar to "bring" in English. In fact, by simply adding an "en" to the end of the English word "bring" we have effectively created the same word in German. And we can actually do the exact same thing with a great number of other English words.

For example, let's take the English word "camp"/"to camp". Now, to say "camp" in German, again we can simply add an "en" to the end of the English word "camp". Let's try that now: take the English word "camp" and add "en" onto the end of it. What does that give you?

campen
(camp-urn)

And this means "camp" in German.

Let's try another example, doing exactly the same thing, but this time let's use the English word "park" / "to park". Again, we'll simply add "en" onto the end of the word "park" and we'll end up with the word that means "park" in German. So, do that now – add "en" onto the end of the English word "park" and tell me, what is the word that means "park" in German?

parken
(park-urn)

And once again, what is "begin" in German?

beginnen
(baig-in-urn)

And what is "bring"?

bringen
(bring-urn)

And what is "park"?

parken
(park-urn)

Finally, what is "camp"?

campen
(camp-urn)

What was "I can" in German?

ich kann
(ikh kan)

So how would you say "I can camp"?

Ich kann campen.
(ikh kan camp-urn)

What is "not" in German?

nicht
(nikht)

And so what is "I can not" / "I cannot"?

ich kann nicht
(ikh kan nikht)

So, how would you say "I cannot camp"?

Ich kann nicht campen.
(ikh kan nikht camp-urn)

How about "I cannot park"?

Ich kann nicht parken.
(ikh kan nikht park-urn)

And "I cannot begin" / "I can't begin"?

Ich kann nicht beginnen.
(ikh kan nikht baig-in-urn)

"She can" in German is:

sie kann
(zee kan)

So how would you say "she can begin"?

Sie kann beginnen.
(zee kan baig-in-urn)

How about "she can camp"?

Sie kann campen.
(zee kan camp-urn)

And so how would you say "she can't camp" / "she cannot camp"?

Sie kann nicht campen.
(zee kan nikht camp-urn)

How about "she can't begin"?

Sie kann nicht beginnen.
(zee kan nikht baig-in-urn)

So, we've got a few of these words now – words like "begin" (beginnen), "camp" (campen), "park" (parken), and "bring" (bringen) – which we've found simply by adding an "en" onto the end of an English word. I want to find one more. This time, we'll try the English word "come". So, just as we did before, we'll take the word "come", and then add "en" onto the end of this, which will hopefully give us the word that means "come" in German. So, take the English word "come" and add "en" onto the end of it. Doing this, what do you get?

Well, if you don't know any German already, you'll probably have arrived at something like "comen".

However, this perhaps is just a bit too English because Germans actually write "come" as:

kommen
(kom-urn)

So, the word is similar to the English, but the spelling and pronunciation are just a bit different, with the German word being pronounced as a "kom" rather than a "kum" sound.

Now again, what is "she can"?

sie kann
(zee kan)

So how would you say "she can come"?

Sie kann kommen.
(zee kan kom-urn)

And how would you say "she can't come"?

Sie kann nicht kommen.
(zee kan nikht kom-urn)

Now again, what is "I can not"?

ich kann nicht
(ikh kan nikht)

So how would you say "I cannot come" / "I can't come"?

Ich kann nicht kommen.
(ikh kan nikht kom-urn)

And what is "she can"?

sie kann
(zee kan)

And how would you say "she can camp"?

Sie kann campen.
(zee kan camp-urn)

The word for "but" in German is:

aber
(ah-ber)

So how would you say "she can camp but…"

Sie kann campen aber…
(zee kan camp-urn ah-ber)

And now try "she can camp but I can't come".

Sie kann campen aber ich kann nicht kommen.
(zee kan camp-urn ah-ber ikh kan nikht kom-urn)

And how about "I can camp but she can't come"?

Ich kann campen aber sie kann nicht kommen.
(ikh kan camp-urn ah-ber zee kan nikht kom-urn)

"Today" in German is:

heute
(hoy-ter)

And again, what is "she can come"?

Sie kann kommen.
(zee kan kom-urn)

Now, if you want to say "she can come today" in German, you will say:

Sie kann heute kommen.
(zee kan hoy-ter kom-urn)

So, literally, this is "she can today come".

Now again, how would you say "she can camp"?

Sie kann campen.
(zee kan camp-urn)

And so how do you think you would say "she can camp today"?

Sie kann heute campen.
(zee kan hoy-ter camp-urn)

So, once again, notice the word order: "she can today camp".

What is "I can" in German?

ich kann
(ikh kan)

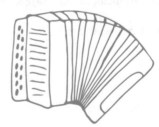

And "I can camp"?

Ich kann campen.
(ikh kan camp-urn)

And so how would you say "I can camp today"?

Ich kann heute campen.
(ikh kan hoy-ter camp-urn)

And how about "I can come today"?

Ich kann heute kommen.
(ikh kan hoy-ter kom-urn)

So the word order is a little different than it is in English. In German, the thing that you can do – whether it's to camp, to come, or whatever – likes to go *at the end*.

Let's try some more examples to make this even clearer.

"Here" in German is:

hier
(hear)

Now again, how would you say "I can camp"?

Ich kann campen.
(ikh kan camp-urn)

So, how do you think you would say "I can camp here"?

Ich kann hier campen.
(ikh kan hear camp-urn)

So, literally, this is "I can here camp". Therefore once again the thing you're going to be doing (camping in this case) goes at the end.

Now, what is "park" / "to park" in German?

parken
(park-urn)

So how would you say "I can park"?

Ich kann parken.
(ikh kan park-urn)

What about "I can park here"?

Ich kann hier parken.
(ikh kan hear park-urn)

"You can" in German is:

du kannst[2]
(doo kanst)

So how would you say "you can park here"?

Du kannst hier parken.
(doo kanst hear park-urn)

How about "you can camp here"?

Du kannst hier campen.
(doo kanst hear kamp-urn)

And what about "you can camp today"?

Du kannst heute campen.
(doo kanst hoy-ter kamp-urn)

"Tonight" in German is literally "today night", which is:

heute Nacht
(hoy-ter nahkht)

So how would you say "you can camp tonight"?

Du kannst heute Nacht campen.
(doo kanst hoy-ter nahkht kamp-urn)

---

2   This is similar to Elizabethan English, where we used to say "thou canst" – a bit outdated in English now of course, unless you're currently reading Shakespeare – for example: "I do protest I never injured thee, But love thee better than thou canst devise." (Romeo and Juliet, Act 3 Scene 1)

So we now know that "you can" is "du kannst". If we want to turn this into a question, we simply reverse the word order just like we do in English, turning "you can" into "can you". Do that now and say "can you?"

Kannst du?
(kanst doo)

So how would you say "can you camp?"

Kannst du campen?
(kanst doo kamp-urn)

How about "can you camp tonight?"

Kannst du heute Nacht campen?
(kanst doo hoy-ter nahkht kamp-urn)

What is "come"?

kommen
(kom-urn)

So, how would you say "can you come tonight?"

Kannst du heute Nacht kommen?
(kanst doo hoy-ter nahkht kom-urn)

"To come over" in German is, more or less, "to come by" (or more literally "to by come"), which is:

vorbeikommen
(for-by-kom-urn)

So, how would you say "can you come over?" / "can you come by?"

Kannst du vorbeikommen?
(kanst doo for-by-kom-urn)

How about "can you come over today?"

Kannst du heute vorbeikommen?
(kanst *doo* hoy-ter for-by-kom-urn)

Finally, how would you say "can you come over tonight?"

Kannst du heute Nacht vorbeikommen?
(kanst *doo* hoy-ter nahkht for-by-kom-urn)

So, you can now construct the sentence that we started the chapter with – and, as you will soon discover, this is only the very beginning of your journey into German!

Building Blocks

You have just learnt how to say (amongst other things) "can you come over tonight?" Having done this, we are now going to move on to expand what you can say through the use of additional "building blocks".

The new building blocks you are going to learn will allow you to begin instantly expanding your range of expression in the German language.

So far, some of the building blocks you have already learnt include:

And you already know how to use these building blocks to construct a sentence. So, once again, how would you say "can you come over tonight?"

So, you already know how to build the four building blocks above into a sentence. Take a look now at the six new building blocks below. Just have a glance over them and then I'll show you how we're going to add these into the mix of what we've learnt so far.

So, here we have six new building blocks to play with.

Now, first things first: please don't to try to memorise them. No, no, no! Instead, I simply want you to play with your building blocks. After all, that's what building blocks are for, isn't it?

And the way you're going to play with them is like this: on the next page they have been put into three piles and all I want you to do is to make sentences with them. You'll do this by each time using one building block from the first pile, one from the second, and one from the third.

You will find that you can say a lot of different things using them in this way and it's up to you what sentences you make. The only thing I want you to make sure you do is to use every building block at least once and, also, please don't bother writing down the sentences you make. Instead, say them out loud, or, if you're not in a place where you can do this, say them in your head. Now, off you go; make as many sentences as you can!

1	2	3
Kannst du (kanst doo) **Can you**	**heute Nacht** (hoy-ter nahkht) **tonight**	**vorbeikommen?** (for-by-kom-um) **come over/to come over/to come by?**
Kann ich (kan ikh) **Can I**	**heute Morgen** (hoy-ter mor-gum) **this morning**	**gehen?** (gay-um) **go/to go?**
Können wir (kum-um veer) **Can we**	**heute Nachmittag** (hoy-ter nahkh-mit-arg) **this afternoon**	**arbeiten?** (ar-bite-um) **work/to work?**

The Checklist

You have now reached the final part of Chapter 1. Once you have finished this short section you will not only have completed your first chapter but you will also understand how this book works as the other chapters follow the same pattern, with your German getting ever more sophisticated as you complete each chapter.

The section you are now on will be the final part of each chapter and is what I call "The Checklist". It involves nothing more than a read-through of a selection of some of the words or expressions you have so far encountered.

You will actually see The Checklist twice. The first time you will see that the German words are written in **black** (on the left-hand side) and that the English words are written in red (on the right-hand side) – and you know what red means... cover up!

So, what I want you to do here is to cover up the English words (which are written in red on the right-hand side) while you read through the list of German words on the left. Read through them all, from the top of the list to the bottom, and see if you can recall what they mean in English (uncover one red word at a time to check if you've remembered the meaning correctly). If you can go through the entire list, giving the correct English meaning for each of the German words /

expressions **without making more than three mistakes in total**, then you're done. If not, then go through the list again. Keep doing this, either working from the top of the list to the bottom or from the bottom to the top (it doesn't matter which) until you can do it **without making more than three mistakes**.

Got it? Then let's go!

Ich kann (ikh kan)	I can
nicht (nikht)	not
beginnen (baig-in-urn)	begin / to begin
Ich kann nicht beginnen. (ikh kan nikht baig-in-urn)	I cannot begin.
parken (park-urn)	park / to park
bringen (bring-urn)	bring / to bring
campen (camp-urn)	camp / to camp
sie kann (zee kan)	she can
kommen (kom-urn)	come / to come
Sie kann kommen. (zee kan kom-urn)	She can come.
Sie kann nicht kommen. (zee kan nikht kom-urn)	She cannot come.
aber (ah-ber)	but
Sie kann campen aber ich kann nicht kommen. (zee kan camp-urn ah-ber ikh kan nikht kom-urn)	She can camp but I can't come.
heute (hoy-ter)	today
Sie kann heute kommen. (zee kan hoy-ter kom-urn)	She can come today.
hier (hear)	here
Ich kann hier campen. (ikh kan hear camp-urn)	I can camp here.
du kannst (doo kanst)	you can
Du kannst hier parken. (doo kanst hear park-urn)	You can park here.
Kannst du? (kanst doo)	Can you?

heute Nacht (hoy-ter nahkht)	tonight
vorbeikommen (for-by-kom-urn)	come over / to come over / to come by
Kannst du heute Nacht vorbeikommen? (kanst doo hoy-ter nahkht for-by-kom-urn)	Can you come over tonight?
Kann ich? (kan ikh)	Can I?
heute Morgen (hoy-ter mor-gurn)	this morning
Kann ich heute Morgen vorbeikommen? (kan ikh hoy-ter mor-gurn for-by-kom-urn)	Can I come over this morning?
Können wir? (kurn-urn veer)	Can we?
heute Nachmittag (hoy-ter nahkh-mit-arg)	this afternoon
gehen (gay-urn)	go / to go
Können wir heute Nachmittag gehen? (kurn-urn veer hoy-ter nahkh-mit-arg gay-urn)	Can we go this afternoon?
arbeiten (ar-bite-urn)	work / to work
Können wir heute Nachmittag arbeiten? (kurn-urn veer hoy-ter nahkh-mit-arg ar-bite-urn)	Can we work this afternoon?

Finished working through that checklist and made less than three mistakes? Yes? Wonderful!

As that's the case, what I now want you to do now is to repeat exactly the same process again below, except that this time you'll be reading through the *English* and trying to recall the German. So, it will be the other way around. So, just relax and work your way up and down the list until you can give the correct German translation for each of the English words / expressions **again without making more than three mistakes in total**. It's not a competition – and I'm not asking you to memorise them. No! Just look at the English words (on the left-hand side) while you cover up the red German words on the right-hand side and see if you can remember how to say them in German. You'll be surprised by how much you get right, even on the first try!

Okay, off you go!

I can	**Ich kann** (ikh kan)
not	**nicht** (nikht)
begin / to begin	**beginnen** (baig-in-urn)
I cannot begin.	**Ich kann nicht beginnen.** (ikh kan nikht baig-in-urn)
park / to park	**parken** (park-urn)
bring / to bring	**bringen** (bring-urn)
camp / to camp	**campen** (camp-urn)
she can	**sie kann** (zee kan)
come / to come	**kommen** (kom-urn)
She can come.	**Sie kann kommen.** (zee kan kom-urn)
She cannot come.	**Sie kann nicht kommen.** (zee kan nikht kom-urn)
but	**aber** (ah-ber)
She can camp but I can't come.	**Sie kann campen aber ich kann nicht kommen.** (zee kan camp-urn ah-ber ikh kan nikht kom-urn)
today	**heute** (hoy-ter)
She can come today.	**Sie kann heute kommen.** (zee kan hoy-ter kom-urn)
here	**hier** (hear)
I can camp here.	**Ich kann hier campen.** (ikh kan hear camp-urn)
you can	**du kannst** (doo kanst)
You can park here.	**Du kannst hier parken.** (doo kanst hear park-urn)
Can you?	**Kannst du?** (kanst doo)
tonight	**heute Nacht** (hoy-ter nahkht)
come over / to come over / to come by	**vorbeikommen** (for-by-kom-urn)

Can you come over tonight?	**Kannst du heute Nacht vorbeikommen?** (kanst doo hoy-ter nahkht for-by-kom-urn)
Can I?	**Kann ich?** (kan ikh)
this morning	**heute Morgen** (hoy-ter mor-gurn)
Can I come over this morning?	**Kann ich heute Morgen vorbeikommen?** (kan ikh hoy-ter mor-gurn for-by-kom-urn)
Can we?	**Können wir?** (kurn-urn veer)
this afternoon	**heute Nachmittag** (hoy-ter nahkh-mit-arg)
go / to go	**gehen** (gay-urn)
Can we go this afternoon?	**Können wir heute Nachmittag gehen?** (kurn-urn veer hoy-ter nahkh-mit-arg gay-urn)
work / to work	**arbeiten** (ar-bite-urn)
Can we work this afternoon?	**Können wir heute Nachmittag arbeiten?** (kurn-urn veer hoy-ter nahkh-mit-arg ar-bite-urn)

Well, that's it, you're done with Chapter 1! Now, don't try to hold on to or remember anything you've learnt here. Everything you learn in earlier chapters will be brought up again and reinforced in later chapters. You don't need to do anything extra or make any effort to memorise anything. The book has been organised so that it does that for you. Now, off you go and have a rest. You've earned it!

Between Chapters Tip!

Between chapters, I'm going to be giving you various tips on language learning. These will range from useful tips about the German language itself to advice on how to fit learning a language in with your daily routine. Ready for the first one? Here it is!

Tip Number One – study (at least a little) every day.

Learning a language is like building a fire – if you don't tend to it, it will go out. So, once you have decided to learn a foreign language, you really should study it every day.

It doesn't have to be for a long time though. Just five or ten minutes each day will be enough, so long as you keep it up. Doing these five or ten minutes will stop you forgetting what you've already learnt and, over time, will let you put more meat on the bones of what you're learning.

As for what counts towards those five or ten minutes, well, that's up to you. Whilst you're working with this book, I would recommend that your five or ten minutes should be spent here, learning with me. Once you're done here, however, your five or ten minutes could be spent reading a German newspaper, watching a German film, or chatting with a German-speaking acquaintance. You could even attend a class if you want to learn in a more formal setting. The important thing though is to make sure that you do a little every day!

CHAPTER 2

I wouldn't like to do
it now because
I'm very busy.

> I wouldn't like to do it now because I'm very busy.

The first chapter has shown you that you can learn how to create full sentences in German with relative ease, even though the word order can be different than in English. It also began to show you how you can change English words into German words, for instance by adding "en" onto the ends of words such as "bring" and "begin".

This is a great way to acquire new vocabulary which, in effect, costs you nothing.

I'm now going to show you an additional way to change English words into German ones in our first **letter swap**...

·Time to swap some letters!
Letter Swap Number 1

Around half of the words in modern English have come into our language via Germanic languages. Using a few simple tricks, you can begin to use these words in German, which will provide you with a large, instant, usable vocabulary. And after all, why bother learning German vocabulary when you can simply invent it!

The first trick we are going to use to start inventing words is to swap the letter "d" in English words for a "t" in German.

So, for instance, if we swap the "**d**" in the English word "har**d**" for a "**t**" we will get the German word for "hard" – which is "har**t**". If we try this again with the English word "un**d**er" we will get the equivalent word in German – "un**t**er". And if we want to say that we "**d**rank" something in German, we can simply say that we "**t**rank" it!

So, swap "d" for "t" to find the German equivalent. Simple!

Now, let's see how we can use these new words to begin expanding our range of expression in German!

In Chapter 1, we created words, like "park", "camp", "begin", and so on, simply by taking English words and adding "en" onto the end of them – and there are, in fact, many more English words that we can also do this with.

For some of them, you simply add an "en" onto the end, as we've already been doing. For others, however, we will also need to make some additional changes — for instance, we might need to use the letter swap above and start changing Ds into Ts!

I'll show you what I mean.

We'll do this the first time with "drink".

Now, we can see that there's a letter "d" at the beginning of "drink". So, let's swap that for a "t".

Do that now and tell me — what do you get?

trink

Good, now let's add an "en" onto the end of this and, by doing so, create the word that means "drink" / "to drink" in German.

So, what will "drink" / "to drink" be in German?

trinken
(trink-urn)

And what is "I can"?

ich kann
(ikh kan)

So how would you say "I can drink"?

Ich kann trinken.
(ikh kan trink-urn)

Turn it into a question now and ask "can I drink?"

Kann ich trinken?
(kan ikh trink-urn)

How about "Can I drink here?"

Kann ich hier trinken?
(kan ikh hear trink-urn)

Converting "drink" into "trinken" has worked out well, so let's try this swapping Ds for Ts trick again. This time, we'll do it with the English word "dance".

So, first of all, let's swap the "d" in "dance" for a "t". What does that give us?

tance

And, as before, to make this into "dance" / "to dance" in German, we will want to add an "en" onto the end.

So, how do you think you would say "dance" / "to dance" in German?

tancen

Good, that's very nearly correct, except that there is just one more thing: German uses a "z" in "dance" instead of a "c". So, change the "c" in "dance" to a "z" and tell me, finally, what is "dance" / "to dance" in German?

tanzen
(tants-urn)

Excellent. So, how would you say "I can dance"?

Ich kann tanzen.
(ikh kan tants-urn)

And "I can dance here"?

Ich kann hier tanzen.
(ikh kan hear tants-urn)

What about "can I dance here?"

Kann ich hier tanzen?
(kan ikh hear tants-urn)

"I would like" in German is:

ich möchte
(ikh murkh-ter)

So how would you say "I would like to dance"?

Ich möchte tanzen.
(ikh murkh-ter tants-urn)

How about "I would like to dance here"?

Ich möchte hier tanzen.
(ikh murkh-ter hear tants-urn)

So, just as before when you were using "can", the thing you're saying that you can or would like to do, whether it's to drink, to dance, or whatever, goes right at the end of the sentence.

What is "today"?

heute
(hoy-ter)

So how would you say "I would like to dance today"?

Ich möchte heute tanzen.
(ikh murkh-ter hoy-ter tants-urn)

"It" in German is:

es
(es)

Now again, what is "I would like"?

ich möchte
(ikh murkh-ter)

So, how would you say "I would like it"?

Ich möchte es.
(ikh murkh-ter es)

What is "to drink"?

trinken
(trink-urn)

So, how would you say "I would like to drink it", keeping in mind that the word meaning "to drink" will still go at the very end?

Ich möchte es trinken.
(ikh murkh-ter es trink-urn)

What is "to bring"?

bringen
(bring-urn)

So how would you say "I would like to bring it"?

Ich möchte es bringen.
(ikh murkh-ter es bring-urn)

And how would you say simply "I would like it"?

Ich möchte es.
(ikh murkh-ter es)

What is "not" in German?

nicht
(nikht)

Now, if you want to say "I wouldn't like it" in German, you will literally say "I would like it not". How would you say that?

Ich möchte es nicht.
(ikh murkh-ter es nikht)

And so how would you say "I wouldn't like to bring it", again keeping in mind that the word meaning "to bring" will still go at the very end of the sentence?

Ich möchte es nicht bringen.
(ikh murkh-ter es nikht bring-urn)

So, literally, this is "I would like it not to bring".

How would you say "I wouldn't like to drink it"?

Ich möchte es nicht trinken.
(ikh murkh-ter es nikht trink-urn)

"To do" in German is:

tun
(toon)

So now say "I wouldn't like to do it".

Ich möchte es nicht tun.
(ikh murkh-ter es nikht toon)

Again, what is "I can"?

ich kann
(ikh kan)

And what is "she can"?

sie kann
(zee kan)

So what is the German word that means "she"?

sie
(zee)

And so how would you say "she would like"?

sie möchte
(zee murkh-ter)

How about "she would like it"?

Sie möchte es.
(zee murkh-ter es)

And "she wouldn't like it"?

Sie möchte es nicht.
(zee murkh-ter es nikht)

And again, what was "to do"?

tun
(toon)

So how would you say "she wouldn't like to do it"?

Sie möchte es nicht tun.
(zee murkh-ter es nikht toon)

And "she wouldn't like to bring it"?

Sie möchte es nicht bringen.
(zee murkh-ter es nikht bring-urn)

How about "she wouldn't like to drink it"?

Sie möchte es nicht trinken.
(zee murkh-ter es nikht trink-urn)

And going back, how would you simply say "she would like it"?

Sie möchte es.
(zee murkh-ter es)

And how would you say "I would like it"?

Ich möchte es.
(ikh murkh-ter es)

What about "I wouldn't like it"?

Ich möchte es nicht.
(ikh murkh-ter es nikht)

Now, once more, what is "today" in German?

heute
(hoy-ter)

47

So how would you say "I wouldn't like it today"?

Ich möchte es nicht heute.
(ikh murkh-ter es nikht hoy-ter)

How about "I wouldn't like to drink it today"?

Ich möchte es nicht heute trinken.
(ikh murkh-ter es nikht hoy-ter trink-urn)

So, even when the sentence has become quite long, the thing that you can or would like to do goes at the end.

How would you say "I wouldn't like to bring it today"?

Ich möchte es nicht heute bringen.
(ikh murkh-ter es nikht hoy-ter bring-urn)

And how about "I wouldn't like to do it today"?

Ich möchte es nicht heute tun.
(ikh murkh-ter es nikht hoy-ter toon)

"Now" in German is:

jetzt
(yetst)

So how would you say "I wouldn't like to do it now"?

Ich möchte es nicht jetzt tun.
(ikh murkh-ter es nikht yetst toon)

What about "I wouldn't like to bring it now"?

Ich möchte es nicht jetzt bringen.
(ikh murkh-ter es nikht yetst bring-urn)

And "I wouldn't like to drink it now"?

Ich möchte es nicht jetzt trinken.
(ikh murkh-ter es nikht yetst trink-urn)

"I am" in German is:

ich bin
(ikh bin)

And "drunk" in German is literally "bedrunken", which is:

betrunken
(be-troon-kurn)

Notice the "d" in the English "drunk" being swapped for a "t" in German.

So, how would you say "I am drunk"?

Ich bin betrunken.
(ikh bin be-troon-kurn)

"Very" in German is:

sehr
(zair)

So how would you say "I am very drunk"?

Ich bin sehr betrunken.
(ikh bin zair be-troon-kurn)

"Romantic" in German is:

romantisch
(roe-marn-tish)

So how would you say "I am romantic"?

Ich bin romantisch.
(ikh bin roe-marn-tish)

How about "I am very romantic"?

Ich bin sehr romantisch.
(ikh bin zair roe-marn-tish)

And how would you say "I am not very romantic"?

Ich bin nicht sehr romantisch.
(ikh bin nikht zair roe-marn-tish)

"Busy" in German is:

beschäftigt
(be-shef-tigt)

So how would you say "I am busy"?

Ich bin beschäftigt.
(ikh bin be-shef-tigt)

What about "I am very busy"?

Ich bin sehr beschäftigt.
(ikh bin zair be-shef-tigt)

And "I am not very busy"?

Ich bin nicht sehr beschäftigt.
(ikh bin nikht zair be-shef-tigt)

And again, how would you say "I am not very drunk"?

Ich bin nicht sehr betrunken.
(ikh bin nikht zair be-troon-kurn)

Catapult Words

You're maybe wondering "what on earth can 'catapult words' possibly be?"

Well, catapult words are words that catapult other words. And where do they catapult them to? To the end of the sentence!

I'll show you what I mean.

To begin with, remind me, how would you say "I am"?

ich bin
(ikh bin)

And so how would you say "I am romantic"?

Ich bin romantisch.
(ikh bin roe-marn-tish)

Okay, that was pretty easy. Now, let's introduce a catapult word and see what it does to this sentence.

Our first catapult word is "because", which in German is:

weil
(vile)

Now again, remind me how you would say "I am romantic"?

Ich bin romantisch.
(ikh bin roe-marn-tish)

And what was "because"?

weil
(vile)

Now, if you want to say "*because* I am romantic" you will quickly discover that "because" acts as a kind of catapult. Don't believe me? Well, watch...

"I am romantic" in German is:

Ich bin romantisch.
(ikh bin roe-marn-tish)

But "*because* I am romantic" in German is:

weil ich romantisch bin
(vile ikh roe-marn-tish bin)

Notice how the "**bin**" (am) has been catapulted to the end of the sentence? Well, this is what catapult words do – they take a word and throw it all the way to the end of the sentence. But that raises an important question of course: how do we know which word it is in this sentence that should be catapulted?

Well, it's very simple, it's the second one.

So again, what is "I am romantic" in German?

Ich bin romantisch.
(ikh bin roe-marn-tish)

So the second word in the sentence is "am" / "bin" and so if we want to add "because" / "weil" to this sentence, this is the word that gets catapulted to the end.

So again, how would you say "because I am romantic"?

weil ich romantisch bin
(vile ikh roe-marn-tish bin)

Now, again, how would you say "I am very romantic"?

Ich bin sehr romantisch.
(ikh bin zair roe-marn-tish)

And how would you say "I am not very romantic"?

Ich bin nicht sehr romantisch.
(ikh bin nikht zair roe-marn-tish)

Now, the second word in this sentence is once again "am" / "bin". So, remembering to catapult it to the end of the sentence, how would you say "because I am not very romantic"?

weil ich nicht sehr romantisch bin
(vile ikh nikht zair roe-marn-tish bin)

Again, what is "drunk"?

betrunken
(be-troon-kurn)

And "I am drunk"?

Ich bin betrunken.
(ikh bin be-troon-kurn)

So how would you say "because I am drunk"?

weil ich betrunken bin
(vile ikh be-troon-kurn bin)

And how about "because I am very drunk"?

weil ich sehr betrunken bin
(vile ikh zair be-troon-kurn bin)

So, as you can see, when we've had a catapult word, such as "weil", it has picked up the second word and thrown it all the way to the end of the sentence. Let's have one more go at doing this!

What is "busy"?

beschäftigt
(be-shef-tigt)

And so how would you say "I am busy"?

Ich bin beschäftigt.
(ikh bin be-shef-tigt)

And "I am very busy"?

Ich bin sehr beschäftigt.
(ikh bin zair be-shef-tigt)

And so how would you say "because I am very busy"?

weil ich sehr beschäftigt bin
(vile ikh zair be-shef-tigt bin)

Excellent!

So, that's how catapult words work. There are a number of other catapult words that exist in German but don't worry because, whenever a catapult word is introduced in this book, I will make sure to let you know that it is one. For the moment though, you only need to know about "because" (weil).

Now, what is "I would like"?

ich möchte
(ikh murkh-ter)

And how would you say "I would like to do it"?

Ich möchte es tun.
(ikh murkh-ter es toon)

How would you say "I wouldn't like to do it"?

Ich möchte es nicht tun.
(ikh murkh-ter es nikht toon)

And "I wouldn't like to do it today"?

Ich möchte es nicht heute tun.
(ikh murkh-ter es nikht hoy-ter toon)

What is "now"?

jetzt
(yetst)

So how would you say "I wouldn't like to do it now"?

Ich möchte es nicht jetzt tun.
(ikh murkh-ter es nikht yetst toon)

And again, how would you say "I am very busy"?

Ich bin sehr beschäftigt.
(ikh bin zair be-shef-tigt)

And, using our catapult word "weil" (because), how would you say "because I am very busy"?

weil ich sehr beschäftigt bin
(vile ikh zair be-shef-tigt bin)

And so, finally, how would you say "I wouldn't like to do it now because I am very busy"?

Ich möchte es nicht jetzt tun, weil ich sehr beschäftigt bin.
(ikh murkh-ter es nikht yetst toon vile ikh zair be-shef-tigt bin)

Well, you've now worked your way back to the sentence we started with and, although we are only at the end of the second chapter, you are already building long, complex sentences in German and beginning to understand how the language works!

Building Blocks 2

As before, it's time to add some new building blocks to the mix. Again, it will be just six new ones. Here they are:

kaufen
(kowf-urn)
buy/to buy

Er möchte
(air murkh-ter)
He would like

bekommen
(be-kom-urn)
get/to get

morgen
(mor-gurn)
tomorrow[3]

später
(shpay-ter)
later

verkaufen
(fair-kowf-urn)
sell/to sell

---

3   "Morgen" is an interesting word. When used on its own it means "tomorrow" but, when used together with another word, it means "morning", such as in "heute Morgen" (this morning). Actually, English isn't so different, since "tomorrow" in English was originally "to-morning". Anyway, don't think too much about any of this, just be aware that "tomorrow" is "morgen" but "heute Morgen" means "this morning".

Once more, these new building blocks have been put into several piles below and what I want you to do is to again make sentences with them, each time using one building block from the first pile, one from the second, one from the third and one from the fourth. Make as many as you can!

Ich möchte
(ikh murkh-ter)
I would like

Sie möchte
(zee murkh-ter)
She would like

Er möchte
(air murkh-ter)
He would like

es
(es)
it

jetzt
(yetst)
now

später
(shpay-ter)
later

morgen
(mor-gurn)
tomorrow

bekommen
(be-kom-urn)
get/to get

kaufen
(kowf-urn)
buy/to buy

verkaufen
(fair-kowf-urn)
sell/to sell

You have now reached your second checklist. Remember, don't skip anything! The checklists are essential if you want what you've learnt to remain in your memory for the long term.

So again, cover up the English words on the right-hand side while you read through the list of German words on the left, trying to recall what they mean in English. If you can go through the entire list, giving the correct English meaning for each of the German words / expressions **without making more than three mistakes in total**, then you're done. If not, then go through the list again. Keep doing this, either working from the top of the list to the bottom or from the bottom to the top (it doesn't matter which) until you can do it **without making more than three mistakes**.

Okay. Ready, set, go!

ich kann (ikh kan)	I can
nicht (nikht)	not
beginnen (baig-in-urn)	begin / to begin
Ich kann nicht beginnen. (ikh kan nikht baig-in-urn)	I cannot begin.
parken (park-urn)	park / to park
bringen (bring-urn)	bring / to bring
campen (camp-urn)	camp / to camp
sie kann (zee kan)	She can
kommen (kom-urn)	come / to come
Sie kann kommen. (zee kan kom-urn)	She can come.
Sie kann nicht kommen. (zee kan nikht kom-urn)	She cannot come.
aber (ah-ber)	but
Sie kann campen aber ich kann nicht kommen. (zee kan camp-urn ah-ber ikh kan nikht kom-urn)	She can camp but I can't come.

heute (hoy-ter)	today
Sie kann heute kommen. (zee kan hoy-ter kom-urn)	She can come today.
hier (hear)	here
Ich kann hier campen. (ikh kan hear camp-urn)	I can camp here.
du kannst (doo kanst)	You can
Du kannst hier parken. (doo kanst hear park-urn)	You can park here.
Kannst du? (kanst doo)	Can you?
heute Nacht (hoy-ter nahkht)	tonight
vorbeikommen (for-by-kom-urn)	come over / to come over / to come by
Kannst du heute Nacht vorbeikommen? (kanst doo hoy-ter nahkht for-by-kom-urn)	Can you come over tonight?
Kann ich? (kan ikh)	Can I?
heute Morgen (hoy-ter mor-gurn)	this morning
Kann ich heute Morgen vorbeikommen? (kan ikh hoy-ter mor-gurn for-by-kom-urn)	Can I come over this morning?
Können wir? (kurn-urn veer)	Can we?
heute Nachmittag (hoy-ter nahkh-mit-arg)	this afternoon
gehen (gay-urn)	go / to go
Können wir heute Nachmittag gehen? (kurn-urn veer hoy-ter nahkh-mit-arg gay-urn)	Can we go this afternoon?
arbeiten (ar-bite-urn)	work / to work
Können wir heute Nachmittag arbeiten? (kurn-urn veer hoy-ter nahkh-mit-arg ar-bite-urn)	Can we work this afternoon?
trinken (trink-urn)	drink / to drink
tanzen (tants-urn)	dance / to dance

ich möchte (ikh murkh-ter)	I would like
sie möchte (zee murkh-ter)	she would like
es (es)	it
tun (toon)	do / to do
jetzt (yetst)	now
ich bin (ikh bin)	I am
betrunken (be-troon-kurn)	drunk
sehr (zair)	very
romantisch (roe-marn-tish)	romantic
beschäftigt (be-shef-tigt)	busy
weil (vile)	because
Kann ich hier trinken? (kan ikh hear trink-urn)	Can I drink here?
Ich möchte hier tanzen. (ikh murkh-ter hear tants-urn)	I would like to dance here.
ich möchte es nicht. (ikh murkh-ter es nikht)	I wouldn't like it.
Ich möchte es nicht bringen. (ikh murkh-ter es nikht bring-urn)	I wouldn't like to bring it.
Ich möchte es nicht heute tun. (ikh murkh-ter es nikht hoy-ter toon)	I wouldn't like to do it today.
Sie möchte es nicht jetzt bringen. (zee murkh-ter es nikht yetst bring-urn)	She wouldn't like to bring it now.
Ich bin sehr betrunken. (ikh bin zair be-troon-kurn)	I am very drunk.
Ich bin nicht sehr romantisch. (ikh bin nikht zair roe-marn-tish)	I am not very romantic.
Ich bin sehr beschäftigt. (ikh bin zair be-shef-tigt)	I am very busy.
weil ich sehr beschäftigt bin (vile ikh zair be-shef-tigt bin)	because I am very busy

Ich möchte es nicht jetzt tun, weil ich sehr beschäftigt bin. (ikh murkh-ter es nikht yetst toon vile ikh zair be-shef-tigt bin)	I wouldn't like to do it now because I am very busy.
Ich möchte es jetzt bekommen. (ikh murkh-ter es yetzt be-kom-urn)	I would like to get it now.
Sie möchte es später kaufen. (zee murkh-ter es shpay-ter kowf-urn)	She would like to buy it later.
Er möchte es morgen verkaufen. (air murkh-ter es mor-gurn fair-kowf-urn)	He would like to sell it tomorrow.

Now, once more, do the same thing again below, except that this time you'll be reading through the list of English words and trying to recall the German. All you need to do is to be able to do one full read-through of them **without making more than 3 mistakes in total** and you're done!

I can	ich kann (ikh kan)
not	nicht (nikht)
begin / to begin	beginnen (baig-in-urn)
I cannot begin.	Ich kann nicht beginnen. (ikh kan nikht baig-in-urn)
park / to park	parken (park-urn)
bring / to bring	bringen (bring-urn)
camp / to camp	campen (camp-urn)
she can	sie kann (zee kan)
come / to come	kommen (kom-urn)
She can come.	Sie kann kommen. (zee kan kom-urn)
She cannot come.	Sie kann nicht kommen. (zee kan nikht kom-urn)
but	aber (ah-ber)
She can camp but I can't come.	Sie kann campen aber ich kann nicht kommen. (zee kan camp-urn ah-ber ikh kan nikht kom-urn)

today	**heute** (hoy-ter)
She can come today.	**Sie kann heute kommen.** (zee kan hoy-ter kom-urn)
here	**hier** (hear)
I can camp here.	**Ich kann hier campen.** (ikh kan hear camp-urn)
you can	**du kannst** (doo kanst)
You can park here.	**Du kannst hier parken.** (doo kanst hear park-urn)
Can you?	**Kannst du?** (kanst doo)
tonight	**heute Nacht** (hoy-ter nahkht)
come over / to come over / to come by	**vorbeikommen** (for-by-kom-urn)
Can you come over tonight?	**Kannst du heute Nacht vorbeikommen?** (kanst doo hoy-ter nahkht for-by-kom-urn)
Can I?	**Kann ich?** (kan ikh)
this morning	**heute Morgen** (hoy-ter mor-gurn)
Can I come over this morning?	**Kann ich heute Morgen vorbeikommen?** (kan ikh hoy-ter mor-gurn for-by-kom-urn)
Can we?	**Können wir?** (kurn-urn veer)
this afternoon	**heute Nachmittag** (hoy-ter nahkh-mit-arg)
go / to go	**gehen** (gay-urn)
Can we go this afternoon?	**Können wir heute Nachmittag gehen?** (kurn-urn veer hoy-ter nahkh-mit-arg gay-urn)
work / to work	**arbeiten** (ar-bite-urn)
Can we work this afternoon?	**Können wir heute Nachmittag arbeiten?** (kurn-urn veer hoy-ter nahkh-mit-arg ar-bite-urn)
drink / to drink	**trinken** (trink-urn)
dance / to dance	**tanzen** (tants-urn)

I would like	ich möchte (ikh murkh-ter)
she would like	sie möchte (zee murkh-ter)
it	es (es)
do / to do	tun (toon)
now	jetzt (yetst)
I am	ich bin (ikh bin)
drunk	betrunken (be-troon-kurn)
very	sehr (zair)
romantic	romantisch (roe-marn-tish)
busy	beschäftigt (be-shef-tigt)
because	weil (vile)
Can I drink here?	Kann ich hier trinken? (kan ikh hear trink-urn)
I would like to dance here.	Ich möchte hier tanzen. (ikh murkh-ter hear tants-urn)
I wouldn't like it.	Ich möchte es nicht. (ikh murkh-ter es nikht)
I wouldn't like to bring it.	Ich möchte es nicht bringen. (ikh murkh-ter es nikht bring-urn)
I wouldn't like to do it today.	Ich möchte es nicht heute tun. (ikh murkh-ter es nikht hoy-ter toon)
She wouldn't like to bring it now.	Sie möchte es nicht jetzt bringen. (zee murkh-ter es nikht yetst bring-urn)
I am very drunk.	Ich bin sehr betrunken. (ikh bin zair be-troon-kurn)
I am not very romantic.	Ich bin nicht sehr romantisch. (ikh bin nikht zair roe-marn-tish)
I am very busy.	Ich bin sehr beschäftigt. (ikh bin zair be-shef-tigt)
because I am very busy	weil ich sehr beschäftigt bin (vile ikh zair be-shef-tigt bin)

I wouldn't like to do it now because I am very busy.	Ich möchte es nicht jetzt tun, weil ich sehr beschäftigt bin. (ikh murkh-ter es nikht yetst toon vile ikh zair be-shef-tigt bin)
I would like to get it now.	Ich möchte es jetzt bekommen. (ikh murkh-ter es yetzt be-kom-urn)
She would like to buy it later.	Sie möchte es später kaufen. (zee murkh-ter es shpay-ter kowf-urn)
He would like to sell it tomorrow.	Er möchte es morgen verkaufen. (air murkh-ter es mor-gurn fair-kowf-urn)

Well, that's it, you're done with Chapter 2! Remember, don't try to hold on to or remember anything you've learnt here. Everything you learn in earlier chapters will be brought back up and reinforced in later chapters. You don't need to do anything or make any effort to memorise anything. The book has been organised in such a way that it will do that for you. So, off you go now and have a rest please!

Stop while you're still enjoying it!

Arnold Schwarzenegger once said that the key to his body building success was that he stopped his workout each day just before it started to get boring. On the few occasions that he went past that point, he found it incredibly hard to return to the gym again the next day – and he *loved* working out.

So, as you will almost certainly recall, Tip 1 suggested that you should study every day – which you definitely should do if you can. But that doesn't mean that you should overdo it. So, if you're not really in the mood, just do five minutes. If you are in the mood though, don't push yourself too hard. Stop before you get to the point where it doesn't feel fun any longer. Best to leave yourself feeling hungry for more rather than bloated and fed up!

CHAPTER 3

I bought the ticket but I didn't see the film.

"I bought the ticket but I didn't see the film."

It's the sort of sentence that you might say in a conversation in English without even thinking about it, but how do we put it together in German? And what lessons will we learn along the way?

Let's find out!

Once again, how would you say "I would like to drink it"?

Ich möchte es trinken.
(ikh murkh-ter es trink-urn)

"The milk" in German is:

die Milch
(dee milkh)

So how would you say "I would like to drink the milk"?

Ich möchte die Milch trinken.
(ikh murkh-ter dee milkh trink-urn)

"The beer" in German is:

das Bier
(das bee-er)

So how would you say "I would like to drink the beer"?

Ich möchte das Bier trinken.
(ikh murkh-ter das bee-er trink-urn)

"Is" in German is:

ist
(ist)

So, how would you say "the beer is…"?

Das Bier ist…
(das bee-er ist)

"Good" in German is:

gut
(goot)

So how would you say "the beer is good"?

Das Bier ist gut.
(das bee-er ist goot)

And how would you say "the milk is good"?

Die Milch ist gut.
(dee milkh ist goot)

Notice how there is more than one word for "the" in German. "The milk" is *die* Milch whereas "the beer" is *das* Bier.

"The wine" in German is:

der Wein
(dair vine)

So how would you say "the wine is good"?

Der Wein ist gut.
(dair vine ist goot)

So, here'

have our third word for "the" in German: "der".

Three words for "the"?

How strange! *Three* words for "the"? Seriously? Why on earth would anyone want that?

Well, yes, it does seem odd to us as English speakers that a language would have more than one word for "the". I mean, what's the point?

Well, to tell you the truth, there really isn't one; it's just a simple reality that we must learn to deal with.

In German, things are classed as either "masculine", "feminine" or "neuter" and the words used for "the" vary according to which of these categories a word belongs to – "der" is used with masculine words, "die" is used with feminine words, and "das" is used with neuter / neutral words.

You could say, of course, that in English we also give things genders – after all, we refer to men and boys as "he", women and girls as "she", and things without any particular gender as "it".

The difference with German though is that it gives genders to *everything* (not just people as in English) and then it uses a different word for "the" to let you know which gender that word is.

So, in German, a man is masculine, yes – but then so is wine. And a woman is feminine, yes – but then so is milk. And of course, beer, as we saw above, is considered (for goodness knows what reason) to be neuter / neutral.

Strange, eh?

Anyway, the secret to dealing with this whole gender business is simply not to waste your time thinking about it! Instead, you will rapidly find that the more you use the language, the more you will know what gender any given word is essentially by instinct. Simply put, using the correct gender will just begin to "sound right". So, as with everything else in this book, all you need to do is to relax and go with the flow – and don't try to memorise anything! Instead, work your way through each chapter and trust in the fact that the content has been organised in such a way that you will pick up the genders of words naturally, along with everything else!

Now there is actually a very specific reason why I'm bothering to teach you about milk and beer and wine, as well as about the fact that there are genders in German and also about how there's more than one word for "the" in German. Yes, there is a reason, I promise! Indeed, there is actually something very important that you need to learn in German that this precise set of drinks (beer, wine and milk) is going to teach you – right now in fact!

First, let's begin with the feminine word "milk". Remind me again, how would you say "the milk is good"?

Die Milch ist gut.
(dee milkh ist goot)

And how would you say "I would like to drink the milk"?

Ich möchte die Milch trinken.
(ikh murkh-ter dee milkh trink-urn)

Well, that was simple, wasn't it? Now let's try a similar sentence but using the neuter word "beer" instead.

So, how would you say "the beer is good"?

Das Bier ist gut.
(das bee-er ist goot)

And how would you say "I would like to drink the beer"?

Ich möchte das Bier trinken.
(ikh murkh-ter das bee-er trink-urn)

So, again, that was simple, wasn't it?

But let's now try the masculine word "wine". Again, how would you say "the wine is good"?

Der Wein ist gut.
(dair vine ist goot)

And so how would you say "I would like to drink the wine"?

Ich möchte den Wein trinken.
(ikh murkh-ter dain vine trink-urn)

Oh dear, what on earth has happened here? Why has "der" become "den"?

Well, this is the important something that I wanted to teach you. As we have already learnt, the masculine word for "the" in German is "der". So, "the wine is good", for instance, is "der Wein ist gut" – simple, yes?

However, in German, the masculine word for "the" (der) can change.

In fact, this happens whenever the "der" word ("der Wein" in this particular instance) is having something done to it – perhaps it is being drunk, eaten, bought, sold, set on fire (it really doesn't matter). When something is done to that "der" word, when it is on the receiving end of some action, the "der" will change to "den". Strange, eh?

Let's try to understand this better by looking at those examples again.

So, once more, how would you say "the wine"?

der Wein
(dair vine)

And how would you say "the wine is good"?

Der Wein ist gut.
(dair vine ist goot)

Notice that "der" does not change here because we're not doing anything with wine – we're not drinking it or pouring it or throwing it away. All we've done is say it is good, we've only described how it is but we haven't done anything to it.

Let's see what happens though when we actually do something to it. Again, try to say "I would like to drink the wine".

Ich möchte den Wein trinken.
(ikh murkh-ter dain vine trink-urn)

So, the moment we talk about what we're going *to do to the wine*, the "der" changes to "den".

Let's try doing something else to it.

Do you remember from the previous checklist how to say "to buy"?

kaufen
(kowf-urn)

So how would you say "I would like to buy the wine"?

Ich möchte den Wein kaufen.
(ikh murkh-ter dain vine kowf-urn)

So, the wine is again having something done to it here, it is being bought, so the word for "the" changes from "der" to "den". As I've already said, however, this change only affects "der" (masculine) words.

Just to prove this, how would you say "I would like to buy the milk"?

Ich möchte die Milch kaufen.
(ikh murkh-ter dee milkh kowf-urn)

So, the feminine word for "the" (die) doesn't change, even when it is having something done to it.

How would you say "I would like to buy the beer"?

Ich möchte das Bier kaufen.
(ikh murkh-ter das bee-er kowf-urn)

Here again, since "beer" is a neuter word, the word for "the" (das) does not change when it is having something done to it.

"The tea" in German is:

der Tee
(dair tay)

So how would you say "I would like to drink the tea"?

Ich möchte den Tee trinken.
(ikh murkh-ter dain tay trink-urn)

So, since we are again dealing with a masculine word, "der" becomes "den", as it does whenever something is *being done to it*.

This may, of course, seem somewhat odd to English speakers – particularly as it only affects masculine words and not feminine or neuter ones – but it is simply how German works.

Anyway, let's forget about all this for a moment – we'll come back to it in a minute anyway – I want us to try another letter swap!

·Time to swap some letters!
Letter Swap Number 2

So, once again, we are going to swap some letters.

In the previous swap, we learnt that you can swap an English letter "d" for a German "t", giving us words like "trinken" (to drink), "tanzen" (to dance), and "betrunken" (drunk).

In this next swap, we're going to be changing Vs into Bs.

So, for instance, if we swap the "**v**" in the English word "ha**v**e" for a "**b**" we will get "ha**b**e" which means "have" in German. If we do this swap again with the "**v**" in the English word "e**v**en" we will get the word for "even" in German – "e**b**en". And if, for example, we try this again with "o**v**er" we will get the German "o**b**er".

So, we can swap **V**s for **B**s and so find the German equivalent. Simple!

Now, let's see how we can use these to begin expanding our range of expression in German.

What is "I would like"?

ich möchte
(ikh murkh-ter)

And which part of that means "I"?

ich
(ikh)

Given that you already know how to say "I" in German, and remembering to swap any "v"s for "b"s, how would you say "I have" in German?

ich habe
(ikh hah-ber)

And so how would you say "I have it"?

Ich habe es.
(ikh hah-ber es)

How about "I don't have it" (literally "I have it not")?

Ich habe es nicht.
(ikh hah-ber es nikht)

"Seen" in German is:

gesehen
(ge-zay-urn)

Now, just as happened with "would like" and "can", the thing that you can or would like to do or have been doing – whether it's drinking, dancing, or seeing something – goes right at the end of the sentence.

So how would you say "I have not seen it" (literally "I have it not seen")?

Ich habe es nicht gesehen.
(ikh hah-ber es nikht ge-zay-urn)

"Done" in German is:

getan
(ge-tarn)

So how would you say "I haven't done it" (literally "I have it not done")?

Ich habe es nicht getan.
(ikh hah-ber es nikht ge-tarn)

And how about "I have done it"?

Ich habe es getan.
(ikh hah-ber es ge-tarn)

And "I have seen it"?

Ich habe es gesehen.
(ikh hah-ber es ge-zay-urn)

What is "because"?

weil
(vile)

Now, try to say "because I have seen it", keeping in mind that "because" will take the second word from "I *have* seen it" and will catapult it all the way to the end of the sentence.

So, how would you say "because I have seen it"?

weil ich es gesehen habe
(vile ikh es ge-zay-urn hah-ber)

How about "because I have not seen it"?

weil ich es nicht gesehen habe
(vile ikh es nikht ge-zay-urn hah-ber)

What is "is" in German?

ist
(ist)

"The film" in German is:

der Film
(dair film)

So how would you say "the film is good"?

Der Film ist gut.
(dair film ist goot)

And how would you say "the film is not good"?

Der Film ist nicht gut.
(dair film ist nikht goot)

How about "the film is not very good"?

Der Film ist nicht sehr gut.
(dair film ist nikht zair goot)

Now again, how would you say "I have seen it"?

Ich habe es gesehen.
(ikh hah-ber es ge-zay-urn)

And again, what does the masculine word for "the" (der) become when it is having something done to it?

den
(dain)

And so, with this in mind, how would you say "I have seen the film"?

Ich habe den Film gesehen.
(ikh hah-ber dain Film ge-zay-urn)

So, once again, we have here a masculine word which, when something is done to it (in this case someone is *seeing* the film) the word for "the" changes from "der" to "den".

As stated previously, however, if you simply want to describe the thing then you don't need to worry about making any changes to "der". So, once more, how would you say "the film is good"?

Der Film ist gut.
(dair film ist goot)

So the "der" does not need to change this time because we're not doing anything to the film – we're not watching it or renting it or buying it. All we've done is said it is good, so we've described how it is but *we haven't done anything to it.*

"The baby" in German is:

das Baby
(das bay-bee)

So, how would you say "I have seen the baby"?

Ich habe das Baby gesehen.
(ikh hah-ber das bay-bee ge-zay-urn)

So, as baby is a "das" / neuter word, the word for "the" does not change, even when it is having something done to it (in this case, it is being seen).

Let's just make this even clearer by giving a still better example. Let's give the baby a kiss!

"Kissed" in German is:

geküsst
(ge-koost)

So how would you say "I have kissed the baby"?

Ich habe das Baby geküsst.
(ikh hah-ber das bay-bee ge-koost)

So, even though the baby is having something done to it (it's being kissed), the word for "the" does not change because it's a "das" / neuter word.

"The mother" in German is:

die Mutter
(dee moo-ter)

So how would you say "I have kissed the mother"?

Ich habe die Mutter geküsst.
(ikh hah-ber dee moo-ter ge-koost)

Again, the mother is on the receiving end of what is happening here – she is the one being kissed – so the word for "the" (die) does not change because it's a "die" / feminine word.

"The father" in German is:

der Vater
(dair far-ter)

So how would you say "I have kissed the father"?

Ich habe den Vater geküsst.
(ikh hah-ber dain far-ter ge-koost)

Now we have a masculine word, "the father", on the receiving end of what is happening and so the word for "the" *does* change, from "der" to "den".

Hopefully this change from "der" to "den" is beginning to feel somewhat familiar.

Of course, in addition to learning how "der" changes to "den", we're also starting to learn how to talk about things in the past in German, to talk about things we have seen and done, and even to say who we have kissed!

And actually one of the rather wonderful things about German is that talking about things that have happened in the past is much easier than it is in English. I'll show you what I mean. Again, how would you say "I have kissed"?

Ich habe geküsst.
(ikh hah-ber ge-koost)

Well, that's great, you now know how to say "I have kissed" but actually "Ich habe geküsst" doesn't only mean "I have kissed". No! It also means "I kissed" and "I did kiss". So what you are actually getting here is three English past tenses for the price of one German one.

I'll show you another example of this. Again, how would you say "I have seen"?

Ich habe gesehen.
(ikh hah-ber ge-zay-urn)

That's good. Now keeping in mind that you get three English past tenses for the price of one German one, how do you think you would say "I saw" in German?

Ich habe gesehen.
(ikh hah-ber ge-zay-urn)

And "I did see"?

Ich habe gesehen.
(ikh hah-ber ge-zay-urn)

So, it's easy: "I have seen", "I saw", and "I did see" can all be expressed by saying "I have seen" (ich habe gesehen) in German. It can count for all three!

Do you remember how to say "I have done"?

Ich habe getan.
(ikh hah-ber ge-tarn)

So, what would be "I did"?

Ich habe getan.
(ikh hah-ber ge-tarn)

And how about "I did do"?

Ich habe getan.
(ikh hah-ber ge-tarn)

And so how would you say "I did do it"?

Ich habe es getan.
(ikh hah-ber es ge-tarn)

And "I did it"?

Ich habe es getan.
(ikh hah-ber es ge-tarn)

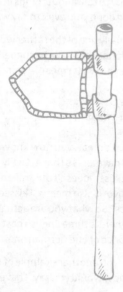

And "I have done it"?

Ich habe es getan.
(ikh hah-ber es ge-tarn)

So, there you have it: three English tenses for the price of one German one.
Awesome!

Now how would you say "I have seen the baby"?

Ich habe das Baby gesehen.
(ikh hah-ber das bay-bee ge-zay-urn)

And so how would you say "I did see the baby"?

Ich habe das Baby gesehen.
(ikh hah-ber das bay-bee ge-zay-urn)

And "I saw the baby"?

Ich habe das Baby gesehen.
(ikh hah-ber das bay-bee ge-zay-urn)

How about "I saw the mother"?

Ich habe die Mutter gesehen.
(ikh hah-ber dee moo-ter ge-zay-urn)

And "I saw the father"?

Ich habe den Vater gesehen.
(ikh hah-ber dain far-ter ge-zay-urn)

Again, notice that, since "the father" is masculine and is having something done to him (in this case he is being seen), the "der" has become "den".

Let's practise the same change again with "the film". What is "the film" in German?

der Film
(dair film)

And so how would you say "I have seen the film"?

Ich habe den Film gesehen.
(ikh hah-ber dain film ge-zay-urn)

How about "I saw the film"?

Ich habe den Film gesehen.
(ikh hah-ber dain film ge-zay-urn)

And "I did see the film"?

Ich habe den Film gesehen.
(ikh hah-ber dain film ge-zay-urn)

"I have bought", "I bought" and "I did buy" in German are all:

Ich habe gekauft.
(ikh hah-ber ge-kowft)

So how would you say "I bought the milk"?

Ich habe die Milch gekauft.
(ikh hah-ber dee milkh ge-kowft)

And what about "I bought the beer"?

Ich habe das Bier gekauft.
(ikh hah-ber das bee-er ge-kowft)

Finally, "I bought the tea"?

Ich habe den Tee gekauft.
(ikh hah-ber dain tay ge-kowft)

"The ticket" in German is:

die Eintrittskarte
(dee ine-trits-kart-er)

This literally means "the entry card".

So how would you say "I have bought the ticket", "I bought the ticket", "I did buy the ticket"?

Ich habe die Eintrittskarte gekauft.
(ikh hah-ber dee ine-trits-kart-er ge-kowft)

Now to say "I did not buy the ticket", "I have not bought the ticket", you will literally say "I have the ticket not bought". How would you say that?

Ich habe die Eintrittskarte nicht gekauft.
(ikh hah-ber dee ine-trits-kart-er nikht ge-kowft)

And again, how would you say "I have seen the film", "I saw the film", "I did see the film"?

Ich habe den Film gesehen.
(ikh hah-ber dain film ge-zay-urn)

And so how would you say "I haven't seen the film", "I didn't see the film" (literally "I have the film not seen")?

Ich habe den Film nicht gesehen.
(ikh hah-ber dain film nikht ge-zay-urn)

What is "but" in German?

aber
(ah-ber)

So how would you say "…but I didn't see the film"?

…aber ich habe den Film nicht gesehen.
(ah-ber ikh hah-ber dain film nikht ge-zay-urn)

And again, how would you say "I bought the ticket"?

Ich habe die Eintrittskarte gekauft.
(ikh hah-ber dee ine-trits-kart-er ge-kowft)

Finally, let's put all this together and express that sentence we started the chapter with. Say "I bought the ticket but I didn't see the film":

Ich habe die Eintrittskarte gekauft, aber ich habe den Film nicht gesehen.
(ikh hah-ber dee ine-trits-kart-er ge-kowft ah-ber ikh hah-ber dain film nikht ge-zay-urn)

Well done! As you can see, you need to understand a number of different factors that are at work if you want to put together a German sentence correctly. Fortunately, you've already learnt several of the most crucial ones. Please enjoy a much deserved break now before going on to learn more tomorrow.

It's time again to add some new building blocks. Here they are:

So, you've got your new building blocks. Make as many sentences as you can!

Checklist 3

You know what to do with the checklist now, so you don't need any reminding about that.

Do bear one thing in mind though. The checklists don't need to be done in one sitting. So, if you get through a page or two and feel that's enough, then simply leave the rest until the next day. Always work at your own pace and don't do so much that you end up feeling overwhelmed. "Steady as she goes" should be your mantra!

ich kann (ikh kan)	I can
nicht (nikht)	not
beginnen (baig-in-urn)	begin / to begin
Ich kann nicht beginnen. (ikh kan nikht baig-in-urn)	I cannot begin.
parken (park-urn)	park / to park
bringen (bring-urn)	bring / to bring
campen (camp-urn)	camp / to camp
sie kann (zee kan)	she can
kommen (kom-urn)	come / to come
Sie kann kommen. (zee kan kom-urn)	She can come.
Sie kann nicht kommen. (zee kan nikht kom-urn)	She cannot come.
aber (ah-ber)	but
Sie kann campen aber ich kann nicht kommen. (zee kan camp-urn ah-ber ikh kan nikht kom-urn)	She can camp but I can't come.
heute (hoy-ter)	today
Sie kann heute kommen. (zee kan hoy-ter kom-urn)	She can come today.
hier (hear)	here
Ich kann hier campen. (ikh kan hear camp-urn)	I can camp here.

du kannst (doo kanst)	you can
Du kannst hier parken. (doo kanst hear park-urn)	You can park here.
Kannst du? (kanst doo)	Can you?
heute Nacht (hoy-ter nahkht)	tonight
vorbeikommen (for-by-kom-urn)	come over / to come over / to come by
Kannst du heute Nacht vorbeikommen? (kanst doo hoy-ter nahkht for-by-kom-urn)	Can you come over tonight?
Kann ich? (kan ikh)	Can I?
heute Morgen (hoy-ter mor-gurn)	this morning
Kann ich heute Morgen vorbeikommen? (kan ikh hoy-ter mor-gurn for-by-kom-urn)	Can I come over this morning?
Können wir? (kurn-urn veer)	Can we?
heute Nachmittag (hoy-ter nahkh-mit-arg)	this afternoon
gehen (gay-urn)	go / to go
Können wir heute Nachmittag gehen? (kurn-urn veer hoy-ter nahkh-mit-arg gay-urn)	Can we go this afternoon?
arbeiten (ar-bite-urn)	work / to work
Können wir heute Nachmittag arbeiten? (kurn-urn veer hoy-ter nahkh-mit-arg ar-bite-urn)	Can we work this afternoon?
trinken (trink-urn)	drink / to drink
tanzen (tants-urn)	dance / to dance
ich möchte (ikh murkh-ter)	I would like
sie möchte (zee murkh-ter)	she would like
es (es)	it
tun (toon)	do / to do
jetzt (yetst)	now

ich bin (ikh bin)	I am
betrunken (be-troon-kurn)	drunk
sehr (zair)	very
romantisch (roe-marn-tish)	romantic
beschäftigt (be-shef-tigt)	busy
weil (vile)	because
Kann ich hier trinken? (kan ikh hear trink-urn)	Can I drink here?
Ich möchte hier tanzen. (ikh murkh-ter hear tants-urn)	I would like to dance here.
Ich möchte es nicht. (ikh murkh-ter es nikht)	I wouldn't like it.
Ich möchte es nicht bringen. (ikh murkh-ter es nikht bring-urn)	I wouldn't like to bring it.
Ich möchte es nicht heute tun. (ikh murkh-ter es nikht hoy-ter toon)	I wouldn't like to do it today.
Sie möchte es nicht jetzt bringen. (zee murkh-ter es nikht yetst bring-urn)	She wouldn't like to bring it now.
Ich bin sehr betrunken. (ikh bin zair be-troon-kurn)	I am very drunk.
Ich bin nicht sehr romantisch. (ikh bin nikht zair roe-marn-tish)	I am not very romantic.
Ich bin sehr beschäftigt. (ikh bin zair be-shef-tigt)	I am very busy.
weil ich sehr beschäftigt bin (vile ikh zair be-shef-tigt bin)	because I am very busy
Ich möchte es nicht jetzt tun, weil ich sehr beschäftigt bin. (ikh murkh-ter es nikht yetst toon vile ikh zair be-shef-tigt bin)	I wouldn't like to do it now because I am very busy.
Ich möchte es jetzt bekommen. (ikh murkh-ter es yetzt be-kom-urn)	I would like to get it now.

Sie möchte es später kaufen. (zee murkh-ter es shpay-ter kowf-urn)	She would like to buy it later.
Er möchte es morgen verkaufen. (air murkh-ter es mor-gurn fair-kowf-urn)	He would like to sell it tomorrow.
gut (goot)	good
die Milch (dee milkh)	the milk
Die Milch ist gut. (dee milkh ist goot)	The milk is good.
Ich möchte die Milch trinken. (ikh murkh-ter dee milkh trink-urn)	I would like to drink the milk.
das Bier (das bee-er)	the beer
Das Bier ist gut. (das bee-er ist goot)	The beer is good.
Ich möchte das Bier trinken. (ikh murkh-ter das bee-er trink-urn)	I would like to drink the beer.
der Wein (dair vine)	the wine
Der Wein ist gut. (dair vine ist goot)	The wine is good.
Ich möchte den Wein trinken. (ikh murkh-ter dain vine trink-urn)	I would like to drink the wine.
kaufen (kowf-urn)	buy / to buy
Ich möchte den Wein kaufen. (ikh murkh-ter dain vine kowf-urn)	I would like to buy the wine.
der Tee (dair tay)	the tea
Ich möchte den Tee trinken. (ikh murkh-ter dain tay trink-urn)	I would like to drink the tea.
ich habe (ikh hah-ber)	I have
Ich habe es. (ikh hah-ber es)	I have it.
Ich habe es nicht. (ikh hah-ber es nikht)	I don't have it.
gesehen (ge-zay-urn)	seen
Ich habe es nicht gesehen. (ikh hah-ber es nikht ge-zay-urn)	I haven't seen it / I didn't see it.
weil ich es nicht gesehen habe (vile ikh es nikht ge-zay-urn hah-ber)	because I haven't seen it / because I didn't see it

getan (ge-tarn)	done
Ich habe es getan. (ikh hah-ber es ge-tarn)	I have done it / I did it / I did do it.
der Film (dair film)	the film
Der Film ist nicht sehr gut. (dair film ist nikht zair goot)	The film is not very good.
Ich habe den Film gesehen. (ikh hah-ber den Film ge-zay-urn)	I have seen the film.
das Baby (das bay-bee)	the baby
die Mutter (dee moo-ter)	the mother
der Vater (dair far-ter)	the father
geküsst (ge-koost)	kissed
Ich habe das Baby geküsst. (ikh hah-ber das bay-bee ge-koost)	I have kissed the baby / I kissed the baby / I did kiss the baby.
gekauft (ge-kowft)	bought
Ich habe den Tee gekauft. (ikh hah-ber dain tay ge-kowft)	I have bought the tea / I bought the tea / I did buy the tea.
die Eintrittskarte (dee ine-trits-kart-er)	the ticket
Ich habe die Eintrittskarte gekauft. (ikh hah-ber dee ine-trits-kart-er ge-kowft)	I have bought the ticket / I bought the ticket / I did buy the ticket.
aber (ah-ber)	but
Ich habe die Eintrittskarte gekauft, aber ich habe den Film nicht gesehen. (ikh hah-ber dee ine-trits-kart-er ge-kowft ah-ber ikh hah-ber dain film nikht ge-zay-urn)	I bought the ticket but I didn't see the film.
Ich habe etwas gekauft. (ikh hah-ber et-vas ge-kowft)	I have bought something / I bought something / I did buy something.
Er hat alles verkauft. (air hat al-ez fur-kowft)	He has sold everything / He sold everything / He did sell everything.
Sie hat nichts gesehen. (zee hat nikhts ge-zay-urn)	She has seen nothing / She saw nothing / She did see nothing.

Now, time to do it the other way around!

I can	**ich kann** (ikh kan)
not	**nicht** (nikht)
begin / to begin	**beginnen** (baig-in-urn)
I cannot begin.	**Ich kann nicht beginnen.** (ikh kan nikht baig-in-urn)
park / to park	**parken** (park-urn)
bring / to bring	**bringen** (bring-urn)
camp / to camp	**campen** (camp-urn)
she can	**sie kann** (zee kan)
come / to come	**kommen** (kom-urn)
She can come.	**Sie kann kommen.** (zee kan kom-urn)
She cannot come.	**Sie kann nicht kommen.** (zee kan nikht kom-urn)
but	**aber** (ah-ber)
She can camp but I can't come.	**Sie kann campen aber ich kann nicht kommen.** (zee kan camp-urn ah-ber ikh kan nikht kom-urn)
today	**heute** (hoy-ter)
She can come today.	**Sie kann heute kommen.** (zee kan hoy-ter kom-urn)
here	**hier** (hear)
I can camp here.	**Ich kann hier campen.** (ikh kan hear camp-urn)
you can	**du kannst** (doo kanst)
You can park here.	**Du kannst hier parken.** (doo kanst hear park-urn)
Can you?	**Kannst du?** (kanst doo)
tonight	**heute Nacht** (hoy-ter nahkht)
come over / to come over / to come by	**vorbeikommen** (for-by-kom-urn)

Can you come over tonight?	Kannst du heute Nacht vorbeikommen? (kanst doo hoy-ter nahkht for-by-kom-urn)
Can I?	Kann ich? (kan ikh)
this morning	heute Morgen (hoy-ter mor-gurn)
Can I come over this morning?	Kann ich heute Morgen vorbeikommen? (kan ikh hoy-ter mor-gurn for-by-kom-urn)
Can we?	Können wir? (kurn-urn veer)
this afternoon	heute Nachmittag (hoy-ter nahkh-mit-arg)
go / to go	gehen (gay-urn)
Can we go this afternoon?	Können wir heute Nachmittag gehen? (kurn-urn veer hoy-ter nahkh-mit-arg gay-urn)
work / to work	arbeiten (ar-bite-urn)
Can we work this afternoon?	Können wir heute Nachmittag arbeiten? (kurn-urn veer hoy-ter nahkh-mit-arg ar-bite-urn)
drink / to drink	trinken (trink-urn)
dance / to dance	tanzen (tants-urn)
I would like	ich möchte (ikh murkh-ter)
she would like	sie möchte (zee murkh-ter)
it	es (es)
do / to do	tun (toon)
now	jetzt (yetst)
I am	ich bin (ikh bin)
drunk	betrunken (be-troon-kurn)
very	sehr (zair)
romantic	romantisch (roe-marn-tish)
busy	beschäftigt (be-shef-tigt)
because	weil (vile)

Can I drink here?	**Kann ich hier trinken?** (kan ikh hear trink-urn)
I would like to dance here.	**Ich möchte hier tanzen.** (ikh murkh-ter hear tants-urn)
I wouldn't like it.	**Ich möchte es nicht.** (ikh murkh-ter es nikht)
I wouldn't like to bring it.	**Ich möchte es nicht bringen.** (ikh murkh-ter es nikht bring-urn)
I wouldn't like to do it today.	**Ich möchte es nicht heute tun.** (ikh murkh-ter es nikht hoy-ter toon)
She wouldn't like to bring it now.	**Sie möchte es nicht jetzt bringen.** (zee murkh-ter es nikht yetst bring-urn)
I am very drunk.	**Ich bin sehr betrunken.** (ikh bin zair be-troon-kurn)
I am not very romantic.	**Ich bin nicht sehr romantisch.** (ikh bin nikht zair roe-marn-tish)
I am very busy.	**Ich bin sehr beschäftigt.** (ikh bin zair be-shef-tigt)
because I am very busy	**weil ich sehr beschäftigt bin** (vile ikh zair be-shef-tigt bin)
I wouldn't like to do it now because I am very busy.	**Ich möchte es nicht jetzt tun, weil ich sehr beschäftigt bin.** (ikh murkh-ter es nikht yetst toon vile ikh zair be-shef-tigt bin)
I would like to get it now.	**Ich möchte es jetzt bekommen.** (ikh murkh-ter es yetzt be-kom-urn)
She would like to buy it later.	**Sie möchte es später kaufen.** (zee murkh-ter es shpay-ter kowf-urn)
He would like to sell it tomorrow.	**Er möchte es morgen verkaufen.** (air murkh-ter es mor-gurn fair-kowf-urn)
good	**gut** (goot)
the milk	**die Milch** (dee milkh)

The milk is good.	Die Milch ist gut. (dee milkh ist goot)
I would like to drink the milk.	Ich möchte die Milch trinken. (ikh murkh-ter dee milkh trink-urn)
the beer	das Bier (das bee-er)
The beer is good.	Das Bier ist gut. (das bee-er ist goot)
I would like to drink the beer.	Ich möchte das Bier trinken. (ikh murkh-ter das bee-er trink-urn)
the wine	der Wein (dair vine)
The wine is good.	Der Wein ist gut. (dair vine ist goot)
I would like to drink the wine.	Ich möchte den Wein trinken. (ikh murkh-ter dain vine trink-urn)
buy / to buy	kaufen (kowf-urn)
I would like to buy the wine.	Ich möchte den Wein kaufen. (ikh murkh-ter dain vine kowf-urn)
the tea	der Tee (dair tay)
I would like to drink the tea.	Ich möchte den Tee trinken. (ikh murkh-ter dain tay trink-urn)
I have	ich habe (ikh hah-ber)
I have it.	Ich habe es. (ikh hah-ber es)
I don't have it.	Ich habe es nicht. (ikh hah-ber es nikht)
seen	gesehen (ge-zay-urn)
I haven't seen it / I didn't see it.	Ich habe es nicht gesehen. (ikh hah-ber es nikht ge-zay-urn)
because I haven't seen it / because I didn't see it	weil ich es nicht gesehen habe (vile ikh es nikht ge-zay-urn hah-ber)
done	getan (ge-tarn)
I have done it / I did it / I did do it.	Ich habe es getan. (ikh hah-ber es ge-tarn)
the film	der Film (dair film)
The film is not very good.	Der Film ist nicht sehr gut. (dair film ist nikht zair goot)
I have seen the film.	Ich habe den Film gesehen. (ikh hah-ber den Film ge-zay-urn)

the baby	das Baby (das bay-bee)
the mother	die Mutter (dee moo-ter)
the father	der Vater (dair far-ter)
kissed	geküsst (ge-koost)
I have kissed the baby / I kissed the baby / I did kiss the baby.	Ich habe das Baby geküsst. (ikh hah-ber das bay-bee ge-koost)
bought	gekauft (ge-kowft)
I have bought the tea / I bought the tea / I did buy the tea.	Ich habe den Tee gekauft. (ikh hah-ber dain tay ge-kowft)
the ticket	die Eintrittskarte (dee ine-trits-kart-er)
I have bought the ticket / I bought the ticket / I did buy the ticket.	Ich habe die Eintrittskarte gekauft. (ikh hah-ber dee ine-trits-kart-er ge-kowft)
but	aber (ah-ber)
I bought the ticket but I didn't see the film.	Ich habe die Eintrittskarte gekauft, aber ich habe den Film nicht gesehen. (ikh hah-ber dee ine-trits-kart-er ge-kowft ah-ber ikh hah-ber dain film nikht ge-zay-urn)
I have bought something / I bought something / I did buy something.	Ich habe etwas gekauft. (ikh hah-ber et-vas ge-kowft)
He has sold everything / He sold everything / He did sell everything.	Er hat alles verkauft. (air hat al-ez fur-kowft)
She has seen nothing / She saw nothing / She did see nothing.	Sie hat nichts gesehen. (zee hat nikhts ge-zay-urn)

Well, that's it, you're done with Chapter 3. Take a break!

How to learn the German days of the week in an easy and meaningful way!

Do you know the days of the week in German?

Well, whether you do or don't, most people are not aware of what the days of the week actually mean in German – or in English for that matter! If they were, they might be surprised how much easier to remember they become...

Let's take a look at them!

Monday – Montag

Monday, in English, actually means "Moon's Day" and the same is true for German. The Germans use their word for moon, which is "Mond", remove the "d", and add the German word for "day" (Tag) onto the end of it, giving us "Montag" – Moon's Day / Monday.

Tuesday – Dienstag

Tuesday, in English, is dedicated to the one-handed Norse God "Týr" – so Tuesday in English is, in effect, "Týr's Day". Germans dedicate Tuesday to "Týr" as well. But because an English "T" can be swapped for a "D" in German, the German word for Tuesday starts with a "D" instead. So "Týr's Day" in German ends up as "Dienstag" – Týr's Day / Tuesday.

Wednesday – Mittwoch

Ah, here we are now at Wednesday or "Wodan's Day" as it really should read in English. However, whereas in English Wednesday celebrates the god Wodan, in German it simply celebrates the fact that it's the middle of the week, making Wednesday in German "Mittwoch" – quite literally "midweek".

Thursday – Donnerstag

In English, the day after Wodan's Day is Thor's Day, now written Thursday. In German, it is exactly the same. "Thor" in German mythology, however, is called "Donar" and so Thursday in German becomes "Donnerstag" – Donar's Day / Thor's Day.

Friday – Freitag

Friday in English means "Frigga's Day". "Who is Frigga?" you may ask. Well, she was Odin's wife and Thor's mother. She was also, for the earliest English people, the goddess of love. The same was true for the Germans, making Friday in German very easy for English speakers to remember – "Freitag".

Saturday – Samstag

Saturday in English is Saturn's day. The German for Saturday, however, comes from words that in old German meant "sabbath day", as the sabbath was originally observed on Saturday rather than Sunday. Saturday in German is therefore "Samstag".

Sunday – Sonntag

I'm sure you can guess the meaning of Sunday in English; clearly it is the Sun's Day. And the same is true in German. "Sun" in German is "Sonne" and so Sunday becomes "Sonntag".

So, there we have the days of week in German. Hopefully they hold a little more meaning for you than they did before. If you don't know them already, you'll find them on a quick reference list on the next page. Just take a look at it each time you finish a chapter, covering up the German and seeing if you can recall it, and you'll soon pick them up.

Monday	Moon's Day	Montag	
Tuesday	Tyr's Day	Dienstag	
Wednesday	Midweek	Mittwoch	
Thursday	Thor's Day	Donnerstag	
Friday	Frigga's Day	Freitag	
Saturday	Sabbath Day	Samstag	
Sunday	Sun's Day	Sonntag	

CHAPTER 4

I gave the money to the taxi driver.

Well, here we are again. Another chapter, beginning with another simple sentence:

"I gave the money to the taxi driver." This sentence has some very useful stuff in it, but as before, even if you know some German already, you may still struggle with a sentence that seems basic in English but that requires a bit of guidance to construct in German.

"Given" in German is:

gegeben
(*ge-gaib-urn*)

So, how would you say "I have given"?

ich habe gegeben
(ikh hah-ber ge-gaib-urn)

And how would you say "I gave" or "I did give"?

ich habe gegeben
(ikh hah-ber ge-gaib-urn)

So, once again, we're getting three English past tenses for the price of one German one.

"The money" in German is:

das Geld
(das gelt)

So how would you say "I have given the money"?

Ich habe das Geld gegeben.
(ikh hah-ber das gelt ge-gaib-urn)

"The taxi driver" in German is:

der Taxifahrer
(dair taxi-far-er)

Notice how this word is made up of two words that are also in English. "Taxi" is of course a familiar word but "fahrer", meaning "driver" is also familiar to us as English speakers. For example, someone who "drives" over the sea in English is known as a "seafarer" – a "sea-driver" or "sea-traveller" if you like. And, in fact, even someone who "drives" themselves about on their feet in English can be called a "wayfarer".

So, a taxi driver in German is effectively a taxi farer or, as it's spelled in German, a "Taxifahrer".

So, now that you know all about the word for "taxi driver" in German, how would you say "the taxi driver is good"?

Der Taxifahrer ist gut.
(dair taxi-far-er ist goot)

And how about "the taxi driver is drunk"?

Der Taxifahrer ist betrunken.
(dair taxi-far-er ist be-troon-kurn)

And "the taxi driver is busy"?

Der Taxifahrer ist beschäftigt.
(dair taxi-far-er ist be-shef-tigt)

So, above we have very effectively described the taxi driver as "good", "drunk", and "busy". Now let's see what happens if we do something to the taxi driver. Again, what is "seen"?

gesehen
(ge-zay-urn)

So how would you say "I have seen"?

ich habe gesehen
(ikh hah-ber ge-zay-urn)

Now try "I have seen the taxi driver".

Ich habe den Taxifahrer gesehen.
(ikh hah-ber dain taxi-far-er ge-zay-urn)

So, when "the taxi driver" is being seen, the "der" changes to "den".

So how would you say "I have kissed the taxi driver"?

Ich habe den Taxifahrer geküsst.
(ikh hah-ber dain taxi-far-er ge-koost)

Good. So, we are very familiar with what happens to something masculine when something is done to it ("der" changes to "den").

Once more, what is "the money"?

das Geld
(das gelt)

And how would you say "I have given the money"?

Ich habe das Geld gegeben.
(ikh hah-ber das gelt ge-gaib-urn)

What is "the wine"?

der Wein
(dair vine)

So how would you say "I have given the wine"?

Ich habe den Wein gegeben.
(ikh hah-ber dain vine ge-gaib-urn)

What is "the tea"?

der Tee
(dair tay)

So how would you say "I have given the tea"?

Ich habe den Tee gegeben.
(ikh hah-ber dain tay ge-gaib-urn)

So, as I have said, we are now very familiar with (possibly even sick to death of) how, when a masculine word is having something done to it, the word for "the" changes from "der" to "den".

This is not, however, the only time when the word for "the" can change in German.

For instance, if you want to say "to the" in German the word for "the" will again change. Let me show you how this works.

Again, what is "the taxi driver" in German?

der Taxifahrer
(dair taxi-far-er)

Now, if you want to say "to the taxi driver" in German, you will simply change the word you use for "the".

"To the taxi driver" in German is:

dem Taxifahrer
(**daim** taxi-far-er)

Now again, what is "it" in German?

es
(*es*)

So how would you say "I have given it"?

Ich habe *es* gegeben.
(ikh hah-ber *es* ge-gaib-urn)

And what is "to the taxi driver"?

dem Taxifahrer
(daim taxi-far-er)

So how would you say "I have given it to the taxi driver"?

Ich habe *es* dem Taxifahrer *gegeben*.
(ikh hah-ber *es* daim taxi-far-er ge-gaib-urn)

And how do you think you would say "I have given the tea to the taxi driver"?

Ich habe den Tee dem Taxifahrer *gegeben*.
(ikh hah-ber dain tay daim taxi-far-er ge-gaib-urn)

So, in this sentence, we have two lots of masculine words, "the tea" (der Tee) and "the taxi driver" (der Taxifahrer), each undergoing changes to the word for "the" which allow us to know what role is being played by each of these two things in the sentence.

"The tea" in the sentence is the thing having something done to it (it's the thing being given), so "der Tee" becomes "den Tee". "The taxi driver" is the person having the tea given *to* them, so "the taxi driver" (der Taxifahrer) becomes "*to* the taxi driver" (dem Taxifahrer).

So these different words for "the" actually let you know which thing is being given and who it's being given to.

Let's try another similar sentence but with one key difference.

"Der Taxifahrer" actually only refers to a taxi driver when it's a man. If the taxi driver is a woman then "the taxi driver" in German becomes "die Taxifahrerin" – notice the "in" that's been added onto the end.

So, just to get used to this feminine version of "taxi driver" for a moment. How would you say (referring to a female taxi driver) "the taxi driver is drunk"?

Die Taxifahrerin ist betrunken.
(dee taxi-far-er-in ist be-troon-kurn)

How about "the taxi driver is busy"?

Die Taxifahrerin ist beschäftigt.
(dee taxi-far-er-in ist be-shef-tigt)

And how would you say "I have kissed the taxi driver"?

Ich habe die Taxifahrerin geküsst.
(ikh hah-ber dee taxi-far-er-in ge-koost)

So, since this is a feminine word, the word for "the" stays the same whether it's having something done to it or not.

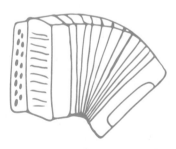

However, if you want to say "*to the* taxi driver" – even for a feminine word – you *will* change the word for "the". So, "to the taxi driver" (when the taxi driver is a woman) in German becomes:

der Taxifahrerin
(dair taxi-far-er-in)

So, how would you say "I gave the tea to the taxi driver"?

Ich habe den Tee der Taxifahrerin gegeben.
(ikh hah-ber dain tay dair taxi-far-er-in ge-gaib-urn)

And how about "I gave the wine to the taxi driver"?

Ich habe den Wein der Taxifahrerin gegeben.
(ikh hah-ber dain vine dair taxi-far-er-in ge-gaib-urn)

So, when you want to say "to the" for a feminine word in German, the "die" changes to "der". When you want to say "to the" for a masculine word the "der" becomes "dem".

I know it seems confusing at this point but so long as you keep building the sentences it will begin to feel easier and, eventually, quite natural. After all, even young German children ultimately master this and they learn it simply by using it when they're little!

So again, just to check what we've done so far:

How would you say "the taxi driver" when the taxi driver is a woman?

die Taxifahrerin
(*dee taxi-far-er-in*)

And how would you say "to the taxi driver" when the driver is a woman?

der Taxifahrerin
(*dair taxi-far-er-in*)

And what is "the taxi driver" when the driver is a man?

der Taxifahrer
(*dair taxi-far-er*)

And how do you say "to the taxi driver" when the driver is a man?

dem Taxifahrer
(*daim taxi-far-er*)

"Das" (neuter) words work in exactly the same way as masculine words when used with "to" in this way.

So, for instance, what is "the baby"?

das Baby
(*das bay-bee*)

"To the baby" in German is:

dem Baby
(*daim bay-bee*)

So how would you say "I have given the milk to the baby" / "I gave the milk to the baby"?

Ich habe die Milch dem Baby gegeben.
(ikh hah-ber dee milkh daim bay-bee ge-gaib-urn)

And how about "I gave the money to the baby"?

Ich habe das Geld dem Baby gegeben.
(ikh hah-ber das gelt daim bay-bee ge-gaib-urn)

Okay. So let's have just one final practice with this "to the" madness.

What is "the baby"?

das Baby
(das bay-bee)

And what is "to the baby"?

dem Baby
(daim bay-bee)

What is "the taxi driver" (male)?

der Taxifahrer
(dair taxi-far-er)

And what is "to the taxi driver" (male)?

dem Taxifahrer
(daim taxi-far-er)

What is "the taxi driver" (female)?

die Taxifahrerin
(dee taxi-far-er-in)

And what is "to the taxi driver" (female)?

der Taxifahrerin
(dair taxi-far-er-in)

Good, that's it, you've got it!

So, finally, returning to the sentence that we began the chapter with, how would you say (when referring to a *female* taxi driver) "I gave the money to the taxi driver"?

Ich habe *das* Geld *der* Taxifahrerin gegeben.
(ikh hah-ber das gelt dair taxi-far-er-in ge-gaib-urn)

And, if you were talking about a *male* taxi driver, how would you say "I gave the money to the taxi driver"?

Ich habe *das* Geld *dem* Taxifahrer gegeben.
(ikh hah-ber das gelt daim taxi-far-er ge-gaib-urn)

So, this sentence – "I gave the money to the taxi driver" – which seems so simple in English, actually contains, and so can help us begin to understand, some of the most complex aspects of German.

As you get used to them, German expressions will start to open up to you, so feel free to practise these last few sentences as many times as you need to in order to feel comfortable with the changes that occur in German to the words for "the". There's no rush, remember, just work through each section at a pace that suits you and then move on to the next part of the book when you're ready – but only when you're ready.

Okay. Building block time. Here they are:

*1 literally "the reckoning"
*2 literally "the maiden"

As before, let's use the building blocks below to make as many sentences as we can. Make sure to use every word at least once and, preferably, several times!

---

4 "The key" in German is "der Schlüssel" but, of course, once it is being "given" or "sent" (as it is in the sentences you can build above) the "der" will become "den".

5 Curiously, "the girl" in German is neuter rather than feminine (it's *das Mädchen*) which is why "to the girl" in German is "*dem Mädchen*" rather than "*der Mädchen*".

Checklist 4

well, off you go then!

ich kann (ikh kan)	I can
nicht (nikht)	not
beginnen (baig-in-urn)	begin / to begin
Ich kann nicht beginnen. (ikh kan nikht baig-in-urn)	I cannot begin.
parken (park-urn)	park / to park
bringen (bring-urn)	bring / to bring
campen (camp-urn)	camp / to camp
sie kann (zee kan)	she can
kommen (kom-urn)	come / to come
Sie kann kommen. (zee kan kom-urn)	She can come.
Sie kann nicht kommen. (zee kan nikht kom-urn)	She cannot come.
aber (ah-ber)	but
Sie kann campen aber ich kann nicht kommen. (zee kan camp-urn ah-ber ikh kan nikht kom-urn)	She can camp but I can't come.
heute (hoy-ter)	today
Sie kann heute kommen. (zee kan hoy-ter kom-urn)	She can come today.
hier (hear)	here
Ich kann hier campen. (ikh kan hear camp-urn)	I can camp here.
du kannst (doo kanst)	you can
Du kannst hier parken. (doo kanst hear park-urn)	You can park here.
Kannst du? (kanst doo)	Can you?
heute Nacht (hoy-ter nahkht)	tonight

vorbeikommen (for-by-kom-urn)	come over / to come over / to come by
Kannst du heute Nacht vorbeikommen? (kanst doo hoy-ter nahkht for-by-kom-urn)	Can you come over tonight?
Kann ich? (kan ikh)	Can I?
heute Morgen (hoy-ter mor-gurn)	this morning
Kann ich heute Morgen vorbeikommen? (kan ikh hoy-ter mor-gurn for-by-kom-urn)	Can I come over this morning?
Können wir? (kurn-urn veer)	Can we?
heute Nachmittag (hoy-ter nahkh-mit-arg)	this afternoon
gehen (gay-urn)	go / to go
Können wir heute Nachmittag gehen? (kurn-urn veer hoy-ter nahkh-mit-arg gay-urn)	Can we go this afternoon?
arbeiten (ar-bite-urn)	work / to work
Können wir heute Nachmittag arbeiten? (kurn-urn veer hoy-ter nahkh-mit-arg ar-bite-urn)	Can we work this afternoon?
trinken (trink-urn)	drink / to drink
tanzen (tants-urn)	dance / to dance
ich möchte (ikh murkh-ter)	I would like
sie möchte (zee murkh-ter)	she would like
es (es)	it
tun (toon)	do / to do
jetzt (yetst)	now
ich bin (ikh bin)	I am
betrunken (be-troon-kurn)	drunk
sehr (zair)	very
romantisch (roe-marn-tish)	romantic
beschäftigt (be-shef-tigt)	busy

weil (vile)	because
Kann ich hier trinken? (kan ikh hear trink-urn)	Can I drink here?
Ich möchte hier tanzen. (ikh murkh-ter hear tants-urn)	I would like to dance here.
Ich möchte es nicht. (ikh murkh-ter es nikht)	I wouldn't like it.
Ich möchte es nicht bringen. (ikh murkh-ter es nikht bring-urn)	I wouldn't like to bring it.
Ich möchte es nicht heute tun. (ikh murkh-ter es nikht hoy-ter toon)	I wouldn't like to do it today.
Sie möchte es nicht jetzt bringen. (zee murkh-ter es nikht yetst bring-urn)	She wouldn't like to bring it now.
Ich bin sehr betrunken. (ikh bin zair be-troon-kurn)	I am very drunk.
Ich bin nicht sehr romantisch. (ikh bin nikht zair roe-marn-tish)	I am not very romantic.
Ich bin sehr beschäftigt. (ikh bin zair be-shef-tigt)	I am very busy.
weil ich sehr beschäftigt bin (vile ikh zair be-shef-tigt bin)	because I am very busy
Ich möchte es nicht jetzt tun, weil ich sehr beschäftigt bin. (ikh murkh-ter es nikht yetst toon vile ikh zair be-shef-tigt bin)	I wouldn't like to do it now because I am very busy.
Ich möchte es jetzt bekommen. (ikh murkh-ter es yetzt be-kom-urn)	I would like to get it now.
Sie möchte es später kaufen. (zee murkh-ter es shpay-ter kowf-urn)	She would like to buy it later.
Er möchte es morgen verkaufen. (air murkh-ter es mor-gurn fair-kowf-urn)	He would like to sell it tomorrow.
gut (goot)	good
die Milch (dee milkh)	the milk

Die Milch ist gut. (dee milkh ist goot)	The milk is good.
Ich möchte die Milch trinken. (ikh murkh-ter dee milkh trink-urn)	I would like to drink the milk.
das Bier (das bee-er)	the beer
Das Bier ist gut. (das bee-er ist goot)	The beer is good.
Ich möchte das Bier trinken. (ikh murkh-ter das bee-er trink-urn)	I would like to drink the beer.
der Wein (dair vine)	the wine
Der Wein ist gut. (dair vine ist goot)	The wine is good.
Ich möchte den Wein trinken. (ikh murkh-ter dain vine trink-urn)	I would like to drink the wine.
kaufen (kowf-urn)	buy / to buy
Ich möchte den Wein kaufen. (ikh murkh-ter dain vine kowf-urn)	I would like to buy the wine.
der Tee (dair tay)	the tea
Ich möchte den Tee trinken. (ikh murkh-ter dain tay trink-urn)	I would like to drink the tea.
ich habe (ikh hah-ber)	I have
Ich habe es. (ikh hah-ber es)	I have it.
Ich habe es nicht. (ikh hah-ber es nikht)	I don't have it.
gesehen (ge-zay-urn)	seen
Ich habe es nicht gesehen. (ikh hah-ber es nikht ge-zay-urn)	I haven't seen it / I didn't see it.
weil ich es nicht gesehen habe (vile ikh es nikht ge-zay-urn hah-ber)	because I haven't seen it / because I didn't see it
getan (ge-tarn)	done
Ich habe es getan. (ikh hah-ber es ge-tarn)	I have done it / I did it / I did do it.
der Film (dair film)	the film
Der Film ist nicht sehr gut. (dair film ist nikht zair goot)	The film is not very good.
Ich habe den Film gesehen. (ikh hah-ber den Film ge-zay-urn)	I have seen the film.

das Baby (das bay-bee)	the baby
die Mutter (dee moo-ter)	the mother
der Vater (dair far-ter)	the father
geküsst (ge-koost)	kissed
Ich habe das Baby geküsst. (ikh hah-ber das bay-bee ge-koost)	I have kissed the baby / I kissed the baby / I did kiss the baby.
gekauft (ge-kowft)	bought
Ich habe den Tee gekauft. (ikh hah-ber dain tay ge-kowft)	I have bought the tea / I bought the tea / I did buy the tea.
die Eintrittskarte (dee ine-trits-kart-er)	the ticket
Ich habe die Eintrittskarte gekauft. (ikh hah-ber dee ine-trits-kart-er ge-kowft)	I have bought the ticket / I bought the ticket / I did buy the ticket.
aber (ah-ber)	but
Ich habe die Eintrittskarte gekauft, aber ich habe den Film nicht gesehen. (ikh hah-ber dee ine-trits-kart-er ge-kowft ah-ber ikh hah-ber dain film nikht ge-zay-urn)	I bought the ticket but I didn't see the film.
Ich habe etwas gekauft. (ikh hah-ber et-vas ge-kowft)	I have bought something / I bought something / I did buy something.
Er hat alles verkauft. (air hat al-ez fur-kowft)	He has sold everything / He sold everything / He did sell everything.
Sie hat nichts gesehen. (zee hat nikhts ge-zay-urn)	She has seen nothing / She saw nothing / She did see nothing.
gegeben (ge-gaib-urn)	given
der Taxifahrer (dair taxi-far-er)	the taxi driver (male)
dem Taxifahrer (daim taxi-far-er)	to the taxi driver (male)
Ich habe den Tee dem Taxifahrer gegeben. (ikh hah-ber dain tay daim taxi-far-er ge-gaib-urn)	I have given the tea to the taxi driver / I gave the tea to the taxi driver / I did give the tea to the taxi driver. (male)

das Geld (das gelt)	the money
Ich habe das Geld dem Taxifahrer gegeben. (ikh hah-ber das gelt daim taxi-far-er ge-gaib-urn)	I have given the money to the taxi driver / I gave the money to the taxi driver / I did give the money to the taxi driver. (male)
die Taxifahrerin (dee taxi-far-er-in)	the taxi driver (female)
der Taxifahrerin (dair taxi-far-er-in)	to the taxi driver (female)
Ich habe den Wein der Taxifahrerin gegeben. (ikh hah-ber dain vine dair taxi-far-er-in ge-gaib-urn)	I have given the wine to the taxi driver / I gave the wine to the taxi driver / I did give the wine to the taxi driver. (female)
Ich habe das Geld der Taxifahrerin gegeben. (ikh hah-ber das gelt dair taxi-far-er-in ge-gaib-urn)	I have given the money to the taxi driver / I gave the money to the taxi driver / I did give the money to the taxi driver. (female)
dem Baby (daim bay-bee)	to the baby
Ich habe die Milch dem Baby gegeben. (ikh hah-ber dee milkh daim bay-bee ge-gaib-urn)	I have given the milk to the baby / I gave the milk to the baby / I did give the milk to the baby.
Ich habe den Schlüssel dem Mädchen gegeben. (ikh hah-ber dain shloos-all dem maid-shen ge-gaib-urn)	I have given the key to the girl / I gave the key to the girl / I did give the key to the girl.
Sie haben die Rechnung dem Taxifahrer geschickt. (zee harb-urn dee rekh-nung daim taxi-far-er ge-shikt)	They have sent the bill to the taxi driver / They sent the bill to the taxi driver / They did send the bill to the taxi driver. (male)
Wir haben das Geld der Taxifahrerin geschickt. (veer harb-urn das gelt dair taxi-far-er-in ge-shikt)	We have sent the money to the taxi driver / We sent the money to the taxi driver / We did send the money to the taxi driver. (female)

Now, time to do it the other way around!

I can	**ich kann** (ikh kan)
not	**nicht** (nikht)
begin / to begin	**beginnen** (baig-in-urn)
I cannot begin.	**Ich kann nicht beginnen.** (ikh kan nikht baig-in-urn)
park / to park	**parken** (park-urn)
bring / to bring	**bringen** (bring-urn)
camp / to camp	**campen** (camp-urn)
she can	**sie kann** (zee kan)
come / to come	**kommen** (kom-urn)
She can come.	**Sie kann kommen.** (zee kan kom-urn)
She cannot come.	**Sie kann nicht kommen.** (zee kan nikht kom-urn)
but	**aber** (ah-ber)
She can camp but I can't come.	**Sie kann campen aber ich kann nicht kommen.** (zee kan camp-urn ah-ber ikh kan nikht kom-urn)
today	**heute** (hoy-ter)
She can come today.	**Sie kann heute kommen.** (zee kan hoy-ter kom-urn)
here	**hier** (hear)
I can camp here.	**Ich kann hier campen.** (ikh kan hear camp-urn)
you can	**du kannst** (doo kanst)
You can park here.	**Du kannst hier parken.** (doo kanst hear park-urn)
Can you?	**Kannst du?** (kanst doo)
tonight	**heute Nacht** (hoy-ter nahkht)
come over / to come over / to come by	**vorbeikommen** (for-by-kom-urn)

Can you come over tonight?	**Kannst du heute Nacht vorbeikommen?** (kanst doo hoy-ter nahkht for-by-kom-urn)
Can I?	**Kann ich?** (kan ikh)
this morning	**heute Morgen** (hoy-ter mor-gurn)
Can I come over this morning?	**Kann ich heute Morgen vorbeikommen?** (kan ikh hoy-ter mor-gurn for-by-kom-urn)
Can we?	**Können wir?** (kurn-urn veer)
this afternoon	**heute Nachmittag** (hoy-ter nahkh-mit-arg)
go / to go	**gehen** (gay-urn)
Can we go this afternoon?	**Können wir heute Nachmittag gehen?** (kurn-urn veer hoy-ter nahkh-mit-arg gay-urn)
work / to work	**arbeiten** (ar-bite-urn)
Can we work this afternoon?	**Können wir heute Nachmittag arbeiten?** (kurn-urn veer hoy-ter nahkh-mit-arg ar-bite-urn)
drink / to drink	**trinken** (trink-urn)
dance / to dance	**tanzen** (tants-urn)
I would like	**ich möchte** (ikh murkh-ter)
she would like	**sie möchte** (zee murkh-ter)
it	**es** (es)
do / to do	**tun** (toon)
now	**jetzt** (yetst)
I am	**ich bin** (ikh bin)
drunk	**betrunken** (be-troon-kurn)
very	**sehr** (zair)
romantic	**romantisch** (roe-marn-tish)
busy	**beschäftigt** (be-shef-tigt)
because	**weil** (vile)

Can I drink here?	Kann ich hier trinken? (kan ikh hear trink-urn)
I would like to dance here.	Ich möchte hier tanzen. (ikh murkh-ter hear tants-urn)
I wouldn't like it.	Ich möchte es nicht. (ikh murkh-ter es nikht)
I wouldn't like to bring it.	Ich möchte es nicht bringen. (ikh murkh-ter es nikht bring-urn)
I wouldn't like to do it today.	Ich möchte es nicht heute tun. (ikh murkh-ter es nikht hoy-ter toon)
She wouldn't like to bring it now.	Sie möchte es nicht jetzt bringen. (zee murkh-ter es nikht yetst bring-urn)
I am very drunk.	Ich bin sehr betrunken. (ikh bin zair be-troon-kurn)
I am not very romantic.	Ich bin nicht sehr romantisch. (ikh bin nikht zair roe-marn-tish)
I am very busy.	Ich bin sehr beschäftigt. (ikh bin zair be-shef-tigt)
because I am very busy	weil ich sehr beschäftigt bin (vile ikh zair be-shef-tigt bin)
I wouldn't like to do it now because I am very busy.	Ich möchte es nicht jetzt tun, weil ich sehr beschäftigt bin. (ikh murkh-ter es nikht yetst toon vile ikh zair be-shef-tigt bin)
I would like to get it now.	Ich möchte es jetzt bekommen. (ikh murkh-ter es yetzt be-kom-urn)
She would like to buy it later.	Sie möchte es später kaufen. (zee murkh-ter es shpay-ter kowf-urn)
He would like to sell it tomorrow.	Er möchte es morgen verkaufen. (air murkh-ter es mor-gurn fair-kowf-urn)
good	gut (goot)
the milk	die Milch (dee milkh)
The milk is good.	Die Milch ist gut. (dee milkh ist goot)

I would like to drink the milk.	Ich möchte die Milch trinken. (ikh murkh-ter dee milkh trink-urn)
the beer	das Bier (das bee-er)
The beer is good.	Das Bier ist gut. (das bee-er ist goot)
I would like to drink the beer.	Ich möchte das Bier trinken. (ikh murkh-ter das bee-er trink-urn)
the wine	der Wein (dair vine)
The wine is good.	Der Wein ist gut. (dair vine ist goot)
I would like to drink the wine.	Ich möchte den Wein trinken. (ikh murkh-ter dain vine trink-urn)
buy / to buy	kaufen (kowf-urn)
I would like to buy the wine.	Ich möchte den Wein kaufen. (ikh murkh-ter dain vine kowf-urn)
the tea	der Tee (dair tay)
I would like to drink the tea.	Ich möchte den Tee trinken. (ikh murkh-ter dain tay trink-urn)
I have	ich habe (ikh hah-ber)
I have it.	Ich habe es. (ikh hah-ber es)
I don't have it.	Ich habe es nicht. (ikh hah-ber es nikht)
seen	gesehen (ge-zay-urn)
I haven't seen it / I didn't see it.	Ich habe es nicht gesehen. (ikh hah-ber es nikht ge-zay-urn)
because I haven't seen it / because I didn't see it	weil ich es nicht gesehen habe (vile ikh es nikht ge-zay-urn hah-ber)
done	getan (ge-tarn)
I have done it / I did it / I did do it.	Ich habe es getan. (ikh hah-ber es ge-tarn)
the film	der Film (dair film)
The film is not very good.	Der Film ist nicht sehr gut. (dair film ist nikht zair goot)
I have seen the film.	Ich habe den Film gesehen. (ikh hah-ber den Film ge-zay-urn)

the baby	das Baby (das bay-bee)
the mother	die Mutter (dee moo-ter)
the father	der Vater (dair far-ter)
kissed	geküsst (ge-koost)
I have kissed the baby / I kissed the baby / I did kiss the baby.	Ich habe das Baby geküsst. (ikh hah-ber das bay-bee ge-koost)
bought	gekauft (ge-kowft)
I have bought the tea / I bought the tea / I did buy the tea.	Ich habe den Tee gekauft. (ikh hah-ber dain tay ge-kowft)
the ticket	die Eintrittskarte (dee ine-trits-kart-er)
I have bought the ticket / I bought the ticket / I did buy the ticket.	Ich habe die Eintrittskarte gekauft. (ikh hah-ber dee ine-trits-kart-er ge-kowft)
but	aber (ah-ber)
I bought the ticket but I didn't see the film.	Ich habe die Eintrittskarte gekauft, aber ich habe den Film nicht gesehen. (ikh hah-ber dee ine-trits-kart-er ge-kowft ah-ber ikh hah-ber dain film nikht ge-zay-urn)
I have bought something / I bought something / I did buy something.	Ich habe etwas gekauft. (ikh hah-ber et-vas ge-kowft)
He has sold everything / He sold everything / He did sell everything.	Er hat alles verkauft. (air hat al-ez fur-kowft)
She has seen nothing / She saw nothing / She did see nothing.	Sie hat nichts gesehen. (zee hat nikhts ge-zay-urn)
given	gegeben (ge-gaib-urn)
the taxi driver (male)	der Taxifahrer (dair taxi-far-er)
to the taxi driver (male)	dem Taxifahrer (daim taxi-far-er)
I have given the tea to the taxi driver / I gave the tea to the taxi driver / I did give the tea to the taxi driver. (male)	Ich habe den Tee dem Taxifahrer gegeben. (ikh hah-ber dain tay daim taxi-far-er ge-gaib-urn)
the money	das Geld (das gelt)

I have given the money to the taxi driver / I gave the money to the taxi driver / I did give the money to the taxi driver. (male)	Ich habe das Geld dem Taxifahrer gegeben. (ikh hah-ber das gelt daim taxi-far-er ge-gaib-urn)
the taxi driver (female)	die Taxifahrerin (dee taxi-far-er-in)
to the taxi driver (female)	der Taxifahrerin (dair taxi-far-er-in)
I have given the wine to the taxi driver / I gave the wine to the taxi driver / I did give the wine to the taxi driver. (female)	Ich habe den Wein der Taxifahrerin gegeben. (ikh hah-ber dain vine dair taxi-far-er-in ge-gaib-urn)
I have given the money to the taxi driver / I gave the money to the taxi driver / I did give the money to the taxi driver. (female)	Ich habe das Geld der Taxifahrerin gegeben. (ikh hah-ber das gelt dair taxi-far-er-in ge-gaib-urn)
to the baby	dem Baby (daim bay-bee)
I have given the milk to the baby / I gave the milk to the baby / I did give the milk to the baby.	Ich habe die Milch dem Baby gegeben. (ikh hah-ber dee milkh daim bay-bee ge-gaib-urn)
I have given the key to the girl / I gave the key to the girl / I did give the key to the girl.	Ich habe den Schlüssel dem Mädchen gegeben. (ikh hah-ber dain shloos-all dem maid-shen ge-gaib-urn)
They have sent the bill to the taxi driver / They sent the bill to the taxi driver / They did send the bill to the taxi driver. (male)	Sie haben die Rechnung dem Taxifahrer geschickt. (zee harb-urn dee rekh-nung daim taxi-far-er ge-shikt)
We have sent the money to the taxi driver / We sent the money to the taxi driver / We did send the money to the taxi driver. (female)	Wir haben das Geld der Taxifahrerin geschickt. (veer harb-urn das gelt dair taxi-far-er-in ge-shikt)

Well, that's it, you're done with Chapter 4! Remember, don't try to hold onto or remember anything you've learnt here. Everything you learnt in earlier chapters will be brought back up and reinforced in later chapters. You don't need to do anything or make any effort to memorise anything.

Use your "hidden moments"

A famous American linguist, Barry Farber, learnt a great part of the languages he spoke during the "hidden moments" he found in everyday life. Such hidden moments might include the time he spent waiting for a train to arrive or for the kids to come out of school, or for the traffic to get moving in the morning. These hidden moments would otherwise have been useless and unimportant in his daily life but, for someone learning a language, they can be some of the most useful minutes of the day.

Breaking up your studies into lots of little bits like this can also be useful as a way to help stop them from feeling like a great effort or from becoming impractical when your life gets especially hectic.

So, keep this book in your pocket whenever you go out and then make use of such "hidden moments" whenever they come along!

CHAPTER 5 (1)

My father's car is old and shabby.

What is it about some dads and their cars? Either they're obsessives who spend their entire weekends polishing them to oblivion or slobs who use them as waste receptacles.

Well, the sentence at the start of this chapter will not only allow you to pass comment on such behaviour but it's also going to introduce a crucial aspect of German to you. So let's get building it!

"It is" in German is:

es ist
(es ist)

So how would you say "it is good"?

Es ist gut.
(es ist goot)

How about "it is romantic"?

Es ist romantisch.
(es ist roe-marn-tish)

"Old" in German is:

alt
(alt)

So how would you say "it is old"?

Es ist alt.
(es ist alt)

"My car" in German is:

mein Auto
(mine ow-toe)

So how would you say "my car is old"?

Mein Auto ist alt.
(mine ow-toe ist alt)

And "my car is good"?

Mein Auto ist gut.
(mine ow-toe ist goot)

Time to swap some letters!
Letter Swap Number 3

Alright, let's try a third letter swap.

This time, we're going to take describing words that end in "y" in English and swap this "y" for an "ig" in German.

So, for instance, if we swap the "**y**" at the end of the English word "hast**y**" for "**ig**" we will get "hast**ig**" which means "hasty" in German. If we do this swap again with the "**y**" at the end of the English word "hungr**y**" we will get the word that means "hungry" in German – "hungr**ig**". We can also do the same with "sand**y**", which becomes "sand**ig**", "frost**y**", which becomes "frost**ig**", and "wind**y**", which becomes "wind**ig**".

So, we find that in German what would be a "y" at the end of a describing word in English will be an "ig" in German. Simple!

Let's see how we can use this to begin expanding our range of expression in German!

"Shabby" in German is:

schäbig
(shay-big)

So how would you say "My car is shabby"?

Mein Auto ist schäbig.
(mine ow-toe ist shay-big)

And again, how would you say "My car is old"?

Mein Auto ist alt.
(mine ow-toe ist alt)

"And" in German is:

und
(oont)

So how would you say "My car is old and shabby"?

Mein Auto ist alt and schäbig.
(mine ow-toe ist alt oont shay-big)

"Dad", or more literally "father", in German is:

Vater
(far-ter)

So how would you say "my father"?

mein Vater
(mine far-ter)

And how would you say "my father is old"?

Mein Vater ist alt.
(mine far-ter ist alt)

Remembering to swap the "y" for an "ig", how would you say "hungry" in German?

hungrig
(hoong-grig)

And so how would you say "my father is hungry"?

Mein Vater ist hungrig.
(mine far-ter ist hoong-grig)

The English word "dreary" used to have the meaning of "sad" or "sorrowful". Although this meaning has been somewhat lost in English, it remains in German.

So, let's try using a couple of the letter swapping techniques we've learnt so far to convert the English word "dreary" into the German word for "sad".

First of all, we'll begin by swapping the "y" at the end of "dreary" for an "ig". Do that now – what do you get?

drearig

Now, we also learnt at the beginning of Chapter 2 that we can swap a "d" in English for a "t" in German. So do that with "drearig" now – what do you get?

trearig

These two letter swaps combined have got us very close to the modern German word for "sad", which is:

traurig
(trow-rig)

You will come across words such as this in German every so often; they are related to English words but have shifted quite a bit over time and it can be interesting to try to rediscover them through letter swaps.

So, anyway, in German, sad = dreary = traurig.

Now that you know this, how would you say "my father is sad"?

Mein Vater ist traurig.
(mine far-ter ist trow-rig)

And again, how would you say "my father is old"?

Mein Vater ist alt.
(mine far-ter ist alt)

We learnt in the previous chapter that the words for "the" in German can change when you want to say "to the".

So, for instance, what is "the taxi driver" (male)?

der Taxifahrer
(dair taxi-far-er)

And what is "to the taxi driver" (male)?

dem Taxifahrer
(daim taxi-far-er)

And what is "the taxi driver" (female)?

die Taxifahrerin
(dee taxi-far-er-in)

And what would be "to the taxi driver" (female)?

der Taxifahrerin
(dair taxi-far-er-in)

And what is "the baby"?

das Baby
(das bay-bee)

And what is "to the baby"?

dem Baby
(daim bay-bee)

What is "the mother" in German?

die Mutter
(dee moo-ter)

So, what would be "to the mother"?

der Mutter
(dair moo-ter)

What is "the father"?

der Vater
(dair far-ter)

So how would you say "to the father"?

dem Vater
(daim far-ter)

So, you are familiar now with these changes caused to "the" when you want to say "to the" in German.

However, these changes to the words for "the" are not only caused when you are saying "to the" in German. These exact same changes can also be caused by certain "trigger words". For instance, the German word for "of" can cause these exact same changes.

"Of" in German is:

von
(fon)

And "von" will cause the exact same changes to the word "the" as occur when you want to say "to the".

Now, what is "the mother"?

die Mutter
(dee moo-ter)

And what is "to the mother"?

der Mutter
(dair moo-ter)

So, how do you think you would say "of the mother"?

von der Mutter
(fon dair moo-ter)

So, the "von" has triggered the same changes that occur when you want to say "to the".

What is "the baby"?

das Baby
(das bay-bee)

And what is "to the baby"?

dem Baby
(daim bay-bee)

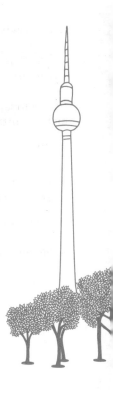

So how would you say "of the baby"?

von dem Baby
(fon daim bay-bee)

Finally, what is "the father"?

der Vater
(dair far-ter)

And what is "to the father"?

dem Vater
(daim far-ter)

And so how would you say "of the father"?

von dem Vater
(fon daim far-ter)

Now, you may well be wondering, why on earth would I want to say "of the mother", "of the baby", "of the father" etc?

Good question.

The answer is that, if you want to say something like "the baby's milk" or "the mother's car" or "the father's beer" in German, then what you will actually say is "the milk of the baby", "the car of the mother" or "the beer of the father".

Let's try doing that now.

Again, what was "the car" in German?

das Auto
(das ow-toe)

And so how would you say "the father's car" (literally "the car of the father")?

das Auto von dem Vater
(das ow-toe fon daim far-ter)

And, pretending it can drive for a moment, "the baby's car"?

das Auto von dem Baby
(das ow-toe fon daim bay-bee)

And what about "the mother's car"?

das Auto von der Mutter
(das ow-toe fon dair moo-ter)

What is "the beer"?

das Bier
(das bee-er)

So how would you say "the mother's beer"?

das Bier von der Mutter
(das bee-er fon dair moo-ter)

What is "the milk"?

die Milch
(dee milkh)

And so how would you say "the baby's milk"?

die Milch von dem Baby
(dee milkh fon daim bay-bee)

And again, how would you say "the father's car"?

das Auto von dem Vater
(das ow-toe fon daim far-ter)

Do you remember how to say "my father" in German?

mein Vater
(mine far-ter)

If you want to say "of my father" in German, the word for "my" will change in the same kind of way that "the" changes.

Again, how did we say "of the father"?

von dem Vater
(fon daim far-ter)

If you want "of my father" you will say:

von meinem Vater
(fon mine-erm far-ter)

So, the change that has happened to "my" matches the change that happened to "the". "Der" became "d**em**" and "mein" has become "mein**em**". Both now end with this same "em".

Now, if you want to say "my father's car" you will simply say "the car of my father" – how would you say that?

das Auto von meinem Vater
(das ow-toe fon mine-erm far-ter)

Now again, how would you say "the baby's car"
(literally "the car of the baby")?

das Auto von dem Baby
(das ow-toe fon daim bay-bee)

So how do you think you would say "*my* baby's car"?

das Auto von meinem Baby
(das ow-toe fon mine-erm bay-bee)

So once more, the change that has happened to "my" matches the change that
happened to "the". "Das" became "d**em**" and so "mein" has become "mein**em**".
Both end with the same "em".

What was "the mother's car" (literally "the car of the mother")?

das Auto von der Mutter
(das ow-toe fon dair moo-ter)

And so how do you think you would say "*my* mother's car"?

das Auto von meiner Mutter
(das ow-toe fon mine-air moo-ter)

And so again, the change that has happened to "my" matches the change that
happened to "the". "Die" became "d**er**" and so "mein" has become "mein**er**".
Both end with the same "er".

What is the German word for "is"?

ist
(ist)

And again, what is "shabby" in German?

schäbig
(shay-big)

And how would you say "old and shabby"?

alt und schäbig
(alt oont shay-big)

So how would you say "my mother's car is old and shabby"?

Das Auto von meiner Mutter ist alt und schäbig.
(das ow-toe fon mine-air moo-ter ist alt oont shay-big)

And how would you say "my father's car is old and shabby"?

Das Auto von meinem Vater ist alt und schäbig.
(das ow-toe fon mine-erm far-ter ist alt oont shay-big)

Excellent! We've now built the sentence that we started with at beginning of the chapter and in the process have begun to understand one of the most crucial aspects of German.

CHAPTER 5 (2)

The car my's father's is old
and shabby. Erm, what?

The car my's father's is old and shabby. Erm, what?

Hmm, that's a weird sentence, isn't it? It has to make you wonder if the author has forgotten how to write in English, let alone how to teach German.

Well, let us hope not!

Actually, the strange way I have written the above sentence will come to make sense in just a few moments and, as it does so, it will allow you to learn what is normally one of the most confusing aspects of German with relative ease.

Let's begin...

What is "the car" in German?

das Auto
(das ow-toe)

And how would you say "my father's car"?

das Auto von meinem Vater
(das ow-toe fon mine-erm far-ter)

So, as we learnt in Part 1 of this chapter, this literally means "the car of my father".

We therefore know that if we want to say who something belongs to we can use this same type of construction. So, "my father's car" becomes "the car of my father", "my baby's milk" becomes "the milk of my baby", and "my mother's wine" becomes "the wine of my mother" and so on.

It is important to be aware of this because otherwise it would be impossible to understand the changes that occur to words like "the" and "my" in German.

And in fact, once you do understand the types of changes that occur to "the" and "my" in German, the language really becomes far easier to learn.

So, just one more time, how would you say "my father's car"?

das Auto von meinem Vater
(das ow-toe fon mine-erm far-ter)

Now, actually, this isn't the only way to say this in German. There is an additional way, which is in fact somewhat similar to the way we would say "my father's car" in English.

In English, we say "my father**'s** car" – notice how we add an "'s" to the end of "father" to show who the car belongs to: it's my father**'s** car.

Well, that same "'s" can be used to show who something belongs to in German. I'll show you how:

First, we'll take the German word for "father" (Vater) and add an "**s**" onto the end it, turning it into "father**'s**". Do that now and tell me, what will "father**'s**" be in German?

Vaters
(far-ters)

Notice how German doesn't bother with an apostrophe here – it's written as Vater**s**, not Vater**'s**.

So, we now know how to say "father's" but if we want to say "my father's car" in German, we also need to add an "s" onto the end of "my", so that we end up effectively saying my's father's.

To do this, remind me, how you would say "my father is hungry"?

Mein Vater ist hungrig.
(mein far-ter ist hoong-grig)

And "my father is old"?

Mein Vater ist alt.
(mine far-ter ist alt)

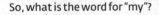

So, what is the word for "my"?

mein
(mine)

Now, we're going to add an "s" onto the end of this "mein". However, "meins" isn't as easy to pronounce as it could be, so in German you actually add "es" to help make the "s" easier to pronounce. So, add "es" onto the end of "mein" now and tell me, what do you end up with?

meines
(mine-es)

And again, what was "father's"?

Vaters
(far-ters)

So how would you say "my's father's"?

meines Vaters
(mine-es far-ters)

Now, to say "my father's car" using this method, you will literally say "the car my's father's". So again, what is "the car"?

das Auto
(das ow-toe)

And what was "my's father's"?

meines Vaters
(mine-es far-ters)

So now put this together and say "my father's car" (literally "the car my's father's").

das Auto meines Vaters
(das ow-toe mine-es far-ters)

Good. Now say "my father's car is old and shabby".

Das Auto meines Vaters ist alt und schäbig.
(das ow-toe mine-es far-ters ist alt oont shay-big)

What is "the baby"?

das Baby
(das bay-bee)

And how would you say "my baby"?

mein Baby
(mine bay-bee)

And how do you think you would say "my's baby's"?

meines Babys
(mine-es bay-bees)

How about "my baby's car"?

das Auto meines Babys
(das ow-toe mine-es bay-bees)

And "my baby's milk"?

die Milch meines Babys
(*dee* milkh mine-es bay-bees)

So, "my baby's milk" as we say it in English, becomes "the milk my's baby's" in German.

Now if you want to say "my mother's milk" or "my mother's wine" or "my mother's car" using this method, it is a bit different. Whereas for neuter we say "my's baby's", and for masculine we say "my's father's", for feminine words, like "mother", you end up with simply "meiner Mutter".

So, how would you say "my mother's car" (literally "the car my's mother")?

das Auto meiner Mutter
(*das* ow-toe mine-air moo-ter)

And how would you say "my mother's car is old"?

Das Auto meiner Mutter ist alt.
(*das* ow-toe mine-air moo-ter ist alt)

And how would you say "my mother's milk"?

die Milch meiner Mutter
(*dee* milkh mine-air moo-ter)

Okay, let's see if we can go through all of these one after another.

How would you say "my father's car"?

das Auto meines Vaters
(*das* ow-toe mine-es far-ters)

And what about "my baby's car"?

das Auto meines Babys
(das ow-toe mine-es bay-bees)

And "my mother's car"?

das Auto meiner Mutter
(das ow-toe mine-air moo-ter)

So, if you have been able to work out those three sentences then you now know how to use what I'll call "the car my's father's" method for saying who something belongs to.

You may well want to go over them again a number of times, however, in order to get them clear in your mind.

Once you've done that, you will be ready to compare them with the alternative way of saying who something belongs to: using "of" (von).

So, using the "von" method, how would you say "my father's car" (literally "the car of my father")?

das Auto von meinem Vater
(das ow-toe fon mine-erm far-ter)

And how about "my baby's car" (literally "the car of my baby")?

das Auto von meinem Baby
(das ow-toe fon mine-erm bay-bee)

And "my mother's car" (literally "the car of my mother")?

das Auto von meiner Mutter
(das ow-toe fon mine-air moo-ter)

So, this is the first method you learnt for saying who something belongs to. Simply use "von" and say "the car of my mother", "the milk of my baby", "the beer of my father", and so on.

The second method we have learnt is what we're calling the "the car my's father's" method. So, using the "the car my's father's" method how would you say "my father's car"?

das Auto meines Vaters
(das ow-toe mine-es far-ters)

And now, using the "von" method, how would you say "my father's car" (literally "the car of my father")?

das Auto von meinem Vater
(das ow-toe fon mine-erm far-ter)

And using the "the car my's father's" method, how would you say "my baby's car"?

das Auto meines Babys
(das ow-toe mine-es bay-bees)

And using the "von" method, how would you say "my baby's car" (literally "the car of my baby")?

das Auto von meinem Baby
(das ow-toe fon mine-erm bay-bee)

And how would you say "my mother's car" using the "the car my's father's" method?

das Auto meiner Mutter
(das ow-toe mine-air moo-ter)

And "my mother's car" using the "von" method?

das Auto von meiner Mutter
(das ow-toe fon mine-air moo-ter)

So, there we have it: two different ways of showing that things belong to someone in German, the "von" method and the "the car my's father's" method.

Understanding them is crucial if you want to be able to speak German properly because, as you will find out whenever you encounter the language, these changes to words such as "the" and "my" affect everything.

Now this can seem overwhelming at first so I recommend, unless you have found it very easy and straightforward the first time around, that you go back over both parts of Chapter 5 several times until all of this begins to feel as though it is in no way confusing.

I should mention, by the way, that the bright side of any initial confusion in this area is that, once you do finally understand it, you discover that you have actually mastered the most difficult aspect of German. Afterwards, accessing the rest of the language is really comparatively easy.

Okay. Building block time. Here they are:

* literally "smutty"

As before, let's use the building blocks below to make as many sentences as we can. Make sure to use every word at least once and, preferably, several times!

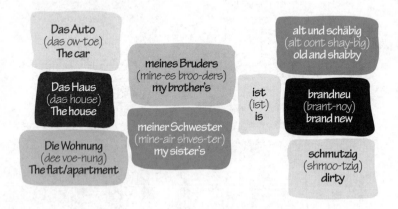

Checklist 5

Well, another chapter finished, another checklist to go through. It's grown very big. Take your time with it. Remember, you don't need to do it all in one go.

ich kann (ikh kan)	I can
nicht (nikht)	not
beginnen (baig-in-urn)	begin / to begin
Ich kann nicht beginnen. (ikh kan nikht baig-in-urn)	I cannot begin.
parken (park-urn)	park / to park
bringen (bring-urn)	bring / to bring
campen (camp-urn)	camp / to camp
sie kann (zee kan)	she can
kommen (kom-urn)	come / to come
Sie kann kommen. (zee kan kom-urn)	She can come.
Sie kann nicht kommen. (zee kan nikht kom-urn)	She cannot come.
aber (ah-ber)	but
Sie kann campen aber ich kann nicht kommen. (zee kan camp-urn ah-ber ikh kan nikht kom-urn)	She can camp but I can't come.
heute (hoy-ter)	today
Sie kann heute kommen. (zee kan hoy-ter kom-urn)	She can come today.
hier (hear)	here
Ich kann hier campen. (ikh kan hear camp-urn)	I can camp here.
du kannst (doo kanst)	You can
Du kannst hier parken. (doo kanst hear park-urn)	You can park here.
Kannst du? (kanst doo)	Can you?
heute Nacht (hoy-ter nahkht)	tonight

vorbeikommen (for-by-kom-urn)	come over / to come over / to come by
Kannst du heute Nacht vorbeikommen? (kanst doo hoy-ter nahkht for-by-kom-urn)	Can you come over tonight?
Kann ich? (kan ikh)	Can I?
heute Morgen (hoy-ter mor-gurn)	this morning
Kann ich heute Morgen vorbeikommen? (kan ikh hoy-ter mor-gurn for-by-kom-urn)	Can I come over this morning?
Können wir? (kurn-urn veer)	Can we?
heute Nachmittag (hoy-ter nahkh-mit-arg)	this afternoon
gehen (gay-urn)	go / to go
Können wir heute Nachmittag gehen? (kurn-urn veer hoy-ter nahkh-mit-arg gay-urn)	Can we go this afternoon?
arbeiten (ar-bite-urn)	work / to work
Können wir heute Nachmittag arbeiten? (kurn-urn veer hoy-ter nahkh-mit-arg ar-bite-urn)	Can we work this afternoon?
trinken (trink-urn)	drink / to drink
tanzen (tants-urn)	dance / to dance
ich möchte (ikh murkh-ter)	I would like
sie möchte (zee murkh-ter)	she would like
es (es)	it
tun (toon)	do / to do
jetzt (yetst)	now
ich bin (ikh bin)	I am
betrunken (be-troon-kurn)	drunk
sehr (zair)	very
romantisch (roe-marn-tish)	romantic
beschäftigt (be-shef-tigt)	busy
weil (vile)	because

Kann ich hier trinken? (kan ikh hear trink-urn)	Can I drink here?
Ich möchte hier tanzen. (ikh murkh-ter hear tants-urn)	I would like to dance here.
Ich möchte es nicht. (ikh murkh-ter es nikht)	I wouldn't like it.
Ich möchte es nicht bringen. (ikh murkh-ter es nikht bring-urn)	I wouldn't like to bring it.
Ich möchte es nicht heute tun. (ikh murkh-ter es nikht hoy-ter toon)	I wouldn't like to do it today.
Sie möchte es nicht jetzt bringen. (zee murkh-ter es nikht yetst bring-urn)	She wouldn't like to bring it now.
Ich bin sehr betrunken. (ikh bin zair be-troon-kurn)	I am very drunk.
Ich bin nicht sehr romantisch. (ikh bin nikht zair roe-marn-tish)	I am not very romantic.
Ich bin sehr beschäftigt. (ikh bin zair be-shef-tigt)	I am very busy.
weil ich sehr beschäftigt bin (vile ikh zair be-shef-tigt bin)	because I am very busy
Ich möchte es nicht jetzt tun, weil ich sehr beschäftigt bin. (ikh murkh-ter es nikht yetst toon vile ikh zair be-shef-tigt bin)	I wouldn't like to do it now because I am very busy.
Ich möchte es jetzt bekommen. (ikh murkh-ter es yetzt be-kom-urn)	I would like to get it now.
Sie möchte es später kaufen. (zee murkh-ter es shpay-ter kowf-urn)	She would like to buy it later.
Er möchte es morgen verkaufen. (air murkh-ter es mor-gurn fair-kowf-urn)	He would like to sell it tomorrow.
gut (goot)	good
die Milch (dee milkh)	the milk
Die Milch ist gut. (dee milkh ist goot)	The milk is good.

Ich möchte die Milch trinken. (ikh murkh-ter dee milkh trink-urn)	I would like to drink the milk.
das Bier (das bee-er)	the beer
Das Bier ist gut. (das bee-er ist goot)	The beer is good.
Ich möchte das Bier trinken. (ikh murkh-ter das bee-er trink-urn)	I would like to drink the beer.
der Wein (dair vine)	the wine
Der Wein ist gut. (dair vine ist goot)	The wine is good.
Ich möchte den Wein trinken. (ikh murkh-ter dain vine trink-urn)	I would like to drink the wine.
kaufen (kowf-urn)	buy / to buy
Ich möchte den Wein kaufen. (ikh murkh-ter dain vine kowf-urn)	I would like to buy the wine.
der Tee (dair tay)	the tea
Ich möchte den Tee trinken. (ikh murkh-ter dain tay trink-urn)	I would like to drink the tea.
ich habe (ikh hah-ber)	I have
Ich habe es. (ikh hah-ber es)	I have it.
Ich habe es nicht. (ikh hah-ber es nikht)	I don't have it.
gesehen (ge-zay-urn)	seen
Ich habe es nicht gesehen. (ikh hah-ber es nikht ge-zay-urn)	I haven't seen it / I didn't see it.
weil ich es nicht gesehen habe (vile ikh es nikht ge-zay-urn hah-ber)	because I haven't seen it / because I didn't see it
getan (ge-tarn)	done
Ich habe es getan. (ikh hah-ber es ge-tarn)	I have done it / I did it / I did do it.
der Film (dair film)	the film
Der Film ist nicht sehr gut. (dair film ist nikht zair goot)	The film is not very good.
Ich habe den Film gesehen. (ikh hah-ber den Film ge-zay-urn)	I have seen the film.
das Baby (das bay-bee)	the baby

die Mutter (dee moo-ter)	the mother
der Vater (dair far-ter)	the father
geküsst (ge-koost)	kissed
Ich habe das Baby geküsst. (ikh hah-ber das bay-bee ge-koost)	I have kissed the baby / I kissed the baby / I did kiss the baby.
gekauft (ge-kowft)	bought
Ich habe den Tee gekauft. (ikh hah-ber dain tay ge-kowft)	I have bought the tea / I bought the tea / I did buy the tea.
die Eintrittskarte (dee ine-trits-kart-er)	the ticket
Ich habe die Eintrittskarte gekauft. (ikh hah-ber dee ine-trits-kart-er ge-kowft)	I have bought the ticket / I bought the ticket / I did buy the ticket.
aber (ah-ber)	but
Ich habe die Eintrittskarte gekauft, aber ich habe den Film nicht gesehen. (ikh hah-ber dee ine-trits-kart-er ge-kowft ah-ber ikh hah-ber dain film nikht ge-zay-urn)	I bought the ticket but I didn't see the film.
Ich habe etwas gekauft. (ikh hah-ber et-vas ge-kowft)	I have bought something / I bought something / I did buy something.
Er hat alles verkauft. (air hat al-ez fur-kowft)	He has sold everything / He sold everything / He did sell everything.
Sie hat nichts gesehen. (zee hat nikhts ge-zay-urn)	She has seen nothing / She saw nothing / She did see nothing.
gegeben (ge-gaib-urn)	given
der Taxifahrer (dair taxi-far-er)	the taxi driver (male)
dem Taxifahrer (daim taxi-far-er)	to the taxi driver (male)
Ich habe den Tee dem Taxifahrer gegeben. (ikh hah-ber dain tay daim taxi-far-er ge-gaib-urn)	I have given the tea to the taxi driver / I gave the tea to the taxi driver / I did give the tea to the taxi driver. (male)
das Geld (das gelt)	the money

Ich habe das Geld dem Taxifahrer gegeben. (ikh hah-ber das gelt daim taxi-far-er ge-gaib-urn)	I have given the money to the taxi driver / I gave the money to the taxi driver / I did give the money to the taxi driver. (male)
die Taxifahrerin (dee taxi-far-er-in)	the taxi driver (female)
der Taxifahrerin (dair taxi-far-er-in)	to the taxi driver (female)
Ich habe den Wein der Taxifahrerin gegeben. (ikh hah-ber dain vine dair taxi-far-er-in ge-gaib-urn)	I have given the wine to the taxi driver / I gave the wine to the taxi driver / I did give the wine to the taxi driver. (female)
Ich habe das Geld der Taxifahrerin gegeben. (ikh hah-ber das gelt dair taxi-far-er-in ge-gaib-urn)	I have given the money to the taxi driver / I gave the money to the taxi driver / I did give the money to the taxi driver. (female)
dem Baby (daim bay-bee)	to the baby
Ich habe die Milch dem Baby gegeben. (ikh hah-ber dee milkh daim bay-bee ge-gaib-urn)	I have given the milk to the baby / I gave the milk to the baby / I did give the milk to the baby.
Ich habe den Schlüssel dem Mädchen gegeben. (ikh hah-ber dain shloos-all dem maid-shen ge-gaib-urn)	I have given the key to the girl / I gave the key to the girl / I did give the key to the girl.
Sie haben die Rechnung dem Taxifahrer geschickt. (zee harb-urn dee rekh-nung daim taxi-far-er ge-shikt)	They have sent the bill to the taxi driver / They sent the bill to the taxi driver / They did send the bill to the taxi driver. (male)
Wir haben das Geld der Taxifahrerin geschickt. (veer harb-urn das gelt dair taxi-far-er-in ge-shikt)	We have sent the money to the taxi driver / We sent the money to the taxi driver / We did send the money to the taxi driver. (female)
Es ist gut. (es ist goot)	It is good.
alt (alt)	old
schäbig (shay-big)	shabby
und (oont)	and
mein Auto (mine ow-toe)	my car
Mein Auto ist alt and schäbig. (mine ow-toe ist alt oont shay-big)	My car is old and shabby.
der Vater (dair far-ter)	The father

traurig (trow-rig)	sad
Mein Vater ist traurig. (mine far-ter ist trow-rig)	My father is sad.
das Bier von dem Vater (das bee-er fon daim far-ter)	the father's beer (VM[*1])
die Milch von dem Baby (dee milkh fon daim bay-bee)	the baby's milk (VM)
das Auto von der Mutter (das ow-toe fon dair moo-ter)	the mother's car (VM)
das Bier von meinem Vater (das bee-er fon mine-erm far-ter)	my father's beer (VM)
die Milch von meinem Baby (dee milkh fon mine-erm bay-bee)	my baby's milk (VM)
das Auto von meiner Mutter (das ow-toe fon mine-air moo-ter)	my mother's car (VM)
das Bier meines Vaters (das bee-er mine-es far-ters)	my father's beer (CMFM[*2])
die Milch meines Babys (dee milkh mine-es bay-bees)	my baby's milk (CMFM)
das Auto meiner Mutter (das ow-toe mine-air moo-ter)	my mother's car (CMFM)
Das Auto von meinem Vater ist alt und schäbig. (das ow-toe fon mine-erm far-ter ist alt oont shay-big)	My father's car is old and shabby. (VM)
Das Auto meines Vaters ist alt und schäbig. (das ow-toe mine-es far-ters ist alt oont shay-big)	My father's car is old and shabby. (CMFM)
Das Haus meines Bruders ist brandneu. (das house mine-es broo-ders ist brant-noy)	My brother's house is brand new. (CMFM)
Die Wohnung meiner Schwester ist schmutzig. (dee voe-nung mine-air shves-ter ist shmootzig)	My sister's flat is dirty. (CMFM)

*1 Using the "von" method

*2 Using the "the car my father's" method

Okay, time for the other way around. Isn't it strange how translating German into English is much easier than translating English into German...

I can	ich kann (ikh kan)
not	nicht (nikht)
begin / to begin	beginnen (baig-in-urn)
I cannot begin.	Ich kann nicht beginnen. (ikh kan nikht baig-in-urn)
park / to park	parken (park-urn)
bring / to bring	bringen (bring-urn)
camp / to camp	campen (camp-urn)
She can	Sie kann (zee kan)
come / to come	kommen (kom-urn)
She can come.	Sie kann kommen. (zee kan kom-urn)
She cannot come.	Sie kann nicht kommen. (zee kan nikht kom-urn)
but	aber (ah-ber)
She can camp but I can't come.	Sie kann campen aber ich kann nicht kommen. (zee kan camp-urn ah-ber ikh kan nikht kom-urn)
today	heute (hoy-ter)
She can come today.	Sie kann heute kommen. (zee kan hoy-ter kom-urn)
here	hier (hear)
I can camp here.	Ich kann hier campen. (ikh kan hear camp-urn)
you can	du kannst (doo kanst)
You can park here.	Du kannst hier parken. (doo kanst hear park-urn)
Can you?	Kannst du? (kanst doo)
tonight	heute Nacht (hoy-ter nahkht)
come over / to come over / to come by	vorbeikommen (for-by-kom-urn)

Can you come over tonight?	Kannst du heute Nacht vorbeikommen? (kanst doo hoy-ter nahkht for-by-kom-urn)
Can I?	Kann ich? (kan ikh)
this morning	heute Morgen (hoy-ter mor-gurn)
Can I come over this morning?	Kann ich heute Morgen vorbeikommen? (kan ikh hoy-ter mor-gurn for-by-kom-urn)
Can we?	Können wir? (kurn-urn veer)
this afternoon	heute Nachmittag (hoy-ter nahkh-mit-arg)
go / to go	gehen (gay-urn)
Can we go this afternoon?	Können wir heute Nachmittag gehen? (kurn-urn veer hoy-ter nahkh-mit-arg gay-urn)
work / to work	arbeiten (ar-bite-urn)
Can we work this afternoon?	Können wir heute Nachmittag arbeiten? (kurn-urn veer hoy-ter nahkh-mit-arg ar-bite-urn)
drink / to drink	trinken (trink-urn)
dance / to dance	tanzen (tants-urn)
I would like	ich möchte (ikh murkh-ter)
she would like	sie möchte (zee murkh-ter)
it	es (es)
do / to do	tun (toon)
now	jetzt (yetst)
I am	ich bin (ikh bin)
drunk	betrunken (be-troon-kurn)
very	sehr (zair)
romantic	romantisch (roe-marn-tish)
busy	beschäftigt (be-shef-tigt)
because	weil (vile)
Can I drink here?	Kann ich hier trinken? (kan ikh hear trink-urn)

I would like to dance here.	**Ich möchte hier tanzen.** (ikh murkh-ter hear tants-urn)
I wouldn't like it.	**Ich möchte es nicht.** (ikh murkh-ter es nikht)
I wouldn't like to bring it.	**Ich möchte es nicht bringen.** (ikh murkh-ter es nikht bring-urn)
I wouldn't like to do it today.	**Ich möchte es nicht heute tun.** (ikh murkh-ter es nikht hoy-ter toon)
She wouldn't like to bring it now.	**Sie möchte es nicht jetzt bringen.** (zee murkh-ter es nikht yetst bring-urn)
I am very drunk.	**Ich bin sehr betrunken.** (ikh bin zair be-troon-kurn)
I am not very romantic.	**Ich bin nicht sehr romantisch.** (ikh bin nikht zair roe-marn-tish)
I am very busy.	**Ich bin sehr beschäftigt.** (ikh bin zair be-shef-tigt)
because I am very busy	**weil ich sehr beschäftigt bin** (vile ikh zair be-shef-tigt bin)
I wouldn't like to do it now because I am very busy.	**Ich möchte es nicht jetzt tun, weil ich sehr beschäftigt bin.** (ikh murkh-ter es nikht yetst toon vile ikh zair be-shef-tigt bin)
I would like to get it now.	**Ich möchte es jetzt bekommen.** (ikh murkh-ter es yetzt be-kom-urn)
She would like to buy it later.	**Sie möchte es später kaufen.** (zee murkh-ter es shpay-ter kowf-urn)
He would like to sell it tomorrow.	**Er möchte es morgen verkaufen.** (air murkh-ter es mor-gurn fair-kowf-urn)
good	**gut** (goot)
the milk	**die Milch** (dee milkh)
The milk is good.	**Die Milch ist gut.** (dee milkh ist goot)
I would like to drink the milk.	**Ich möchte die Milch trinken.** (ikh murkh-ter dee milkh trink-urn)
the beer	**das Bier** (das bee-er)

The beer is good.	Das Bier ist gut. (das bee-er ist goot)
I would like to drink the beer.	Ich möchte das Bier trinken. (ikh murkh-ter das bee-er trink-urn)
the wine	der Wein (dair vine)
The wine is good.	Der Wein ist gut. (dair vine ist goot)
I would like to drink the wine.	Ich möchte den Wein trinken. (ikh murkh-ter dain vine trink-urn)
buy / to buy	kaufen (kowf-urn)
I would like to buy the wine.	Ich möchte den Wein kaufen. (ikh murkh-ter dain vine kowf-urn)
the tea	der Tee (dair tay)
I would like to drink the tea.	Ich möchte den Tee trinken. (ikh murkh-ter dain tay trink-urn)
I have	ich habe (ikh hah-ber)
I have it.	Ich habe es. (ikh hah-ber es)
I don't have it.	Ich habe es nicht. (ikh hah-ber es nikht)
seen	gesehen (ge-zay-urn)
I haven't seen it / I didn't see it.	Ich habe es nicht gesehen. (ikh hah-ber es nikht ge-zay-urn)
because I haven't seen it / because I didn't see it	weil ich es nicht gesehen habe (vile ikh es nikht ge-zay-urn hah-ber)
done	getan (ge-tarn)
I have done it / I did it / I did do it.	Ich habe es getan. (ikh hah-ber es ge-tarn)
the film	der Film (dair film)
The film is not very good.	Der Film ist nicht sehr gut. (dair film ist nikht zair goot)
I have seen the film.	Ich habe den Film gesehen. (ikh hah-ber den Film ge-zay-urn)
the baby	das Baby (das bay-bee)
the mother	die Mutter (dee moo-ter)
the father	der Vater (dair far-ter)
kissed	geküsst (ge-koost)

I have kissed the baby / I kissed the baby / I did kiss the baby.	Ich habe das Baby geküsst. (ikh hah-ber das bay-bee ge-koost)
bought	gekauft (ge-kowft)
I have bought the tea / I bought the tea / I did buy the tea.	Ich habe den Tee gekauft. (ikh hah-ber dain tay ge-kowft)
the ticket	die Eintrittskarte (dee ine-trits-kart-er)
I have bought the ticket / I bought the ticket / I did buy the ticket.	Ich habe die Eintrittskarte gekauft. (ikh hah-ber dee ine-trits-kart-er ge-kowft)
but	aber (ah-ber)
I bought the ticket but I didn't see the film.	Ich habe die Eintrittskarte gekauft, aber ich habe den Film nicht gesehen. (ikh hah-ber dee ine-trits-kart-er ge-kowft ah-ber ikh hah-ber dain film nikht ge-zay-urn)
I have bought something / I bought something / I did buy something.	Ich habe etwas gekauft. (ikh hah-ber et-vas ge-kowft)
He has sold everything / He sold everything / He did sell everything.	Er hat alles verkauft. (air hat al-ez fur-kowft)
She has seen nothing / She saw nothing / She did see nothing.	Sie hat nichts gesehen. (zee hat nikhts ge-zay-urn)
given	gegeben (ge-gaib-urn)
the taxi driver (male)	der Taxifahrer (dair taxi-far-er)
to the taxi driver (male)	dem Taxifahrer (daim taxi-far-er)
I have given the tea to the taxi driver / I gave the tea to the taxi driver / I did give the tea to the taxi driver. (male)	Ich habe den Tee dem Taxifahrer gegeben. (ikh hah-ber dain tay daim taxi-far-er ge-gaib-urn)
the money	das Geld (das gelt)
I have given the money to the taxi driver / I gave the money to the taxi driver / I did give the money to the taxi driver. (male)	Ich habe das Geld dem Taxifahrer gegeben. (ikh hah-ber das gelt daim taxi-far-er ge-gaib-urn)
the taxi driver (female)	die Taxifahrerin (dee taxi-far-er-in)
to the taxi driver (female)	der Taxifahrerin (dair taxi-far-er-in)

I have given the wine to the taxi driver / I gave the wine to the taxi driver / I did give the wine to the taxi driver. (female)	**Ich habe den Wein der Taxifahrerin gegeben.** (ikh hah-ber dain vine dair taxi-far-er-in ge-gaib-urn)
I have given the money to the taxi driver / I gave the money to the taxi driver / I did give the money to the taxi driver. (female)	**Ich habe das Geld der Taxifahrerin gegeben.** (ikh hah-ber das gelt dair taxi-far-er-in ge-gaib-urn)
to the baby	**dem Baby** (daim bay-bee)
I have given the milk to the baby / I gave the milk to the baby / I did give the milk to the baby.	**Ich habe die Milch dem Baby gegeben.** (ikh hah-ber dee milkh daim bay-bee ge-gaib-urn)
I have given the key to the girl / I gave the key to the girl / I did give the key to the girl.	**Ich habe den Schlüssel dem Mädchen gegeben.** (ikh hah-ber dain shloos-all dem maid-shen ge-gaib-urn)
They have sent the bill to the taxi driver / They sent the bill to the taxi driver / They did send the bill to the taxi driver. (male)	**Sie haben die Rechnung dem Taxifahrer geschickt.** (zee harb-urn dee rekh-nung daim taxi-far-er ge-shikt)
We have sent the money to the taxi driver / We sent the money to the taxi driver / We did send the money to the taxi driver. (female)	**Wir haben das Geld der Taxifahrerin geschickt.** (veer harb-urn das gelt dair taxi-far-er-in ge-shikt)
It is good.	**Es ist gut.** (es ist goot)
old	**alt** (alt)
shabby	**schäbig** (shay-big)
and	**und** (oont)
my car	**mein Auto** (mine ow-toe)
My car is old and shabby.	**Mein Auto ist alt and schäbig.** (mine ow-toe ist alt oont shay-big)
the father	**der Vater** (dair far-ter)
sad	**traurig** (trow-rig)
My father is sad.	**Mein Vater ist traurig.** (mine far-ter ist trow-rig)

the father's beer (VM[*1])	das Bier von dem Vater (das bee-er fon daim far-ter)
the baby's milk (VM)	die Milch von dem Baby (dee milkh fon daim bay-bee)
the mother's car (VM)	das Auto von der Mutter (das ow-toe fon dair moo-ter)
my father's beer (VM)	das Bier von meinem Vater (das bee-er fon mine-erm far-ter)
my baby's milk (VM)	die Milch von meinem Baby (dee milkh fon mine-erm bay-bee)
my mother's car (VM)	das Auto von meiner Mutter (das ow-toe fon mine-air moo-ter)
my father's beer (CMFM[*2])	das Bier meines Vaters (das bee-er mine-es far-ters)
my baby's milk (CMFM)	die Milch meines Babys (dee milkh mine-es bay-bees)
my mother's car (CMFM)	das Auto meiner Mutter (das ow-toe mine-air moo-ter)
My father's car is old and shabby. (VM)	Das Auto von meinem Vater ist alt und schäbig. (das ow-toe fon mine-erm far-ter ist alt oont shay-big)
My father's car is old and shabby. (CMFM)	Das Auto meines Vaters ist alt und schäbig. (das ow-toe mine-es far-ters ist alt oont shay-big)
My brother's house is brand new. (CMFM)	Das Haus meines Bruders ist brandneu. (das house mine-es broo-ders ist brant-noy)
My sister's flat is dirty. (CMFM)	Die Wohnung meiner Schwester ist schmutzig. (dee voe-nung mine-air shves-ter ist shmootzig)

That's it. Go and take your well-deserved break!

*1 Using the "von" method
*2 Using the "the car my father's" method

Forget what you were taught at school!

Many of us were told at school that we did not have an aptitude for languages, that we didn't have a "knack" or a "gift" for them.

Well, if this applies to you, then please let me assure you that this is all absolute nonsense! If you are able to read these words in front of you then this demonstrates that you've been able to learn English and, if you can learn one language, then your brain is just as capable of learning another – it simply needs to be approached in the right way!

In fact, if you've got as far as Chapter 5, it should already be obvious to you that you are quite capable of learning a foreign language when it's taught in the right way. The secret to success for you will be choosing the right materials once you're finished with this book (more on that later).

CHAPTER 6 (1)

We're lucky that the weather's
so good.

Person 1:   We're lucky that the weather's so good.

Person 2:   Why?

Person 1:   Because I feel like going to the park.

The brief exchange above does not seem complicated in English and yet, even if you have studied German before, you might well find it impossible to know exactly where to begin in order to express it. By the end of this chapter, you will have learnt how to carry out both sides of this conversation, plus a great deal more German besides.

Let's begin!

Again, what is "I am" in German?

ich bin
(ikh bin)

And how would you say "I am romantic"?

Ich bin romantisch.
(ikh bin roe-marn-tish)

Do you remember what "because" is in German?

weil
(vile)

And do you remember how to say "*because* I am romantic"?

weil ich romantisch bin
(vile ikh roe-marn-tish bin)

So, as we first learnt in Chapter 2, "weil" (because) is a catapult word and we've seen how it took the second word from the original sentence (I *am* romantic) and catapulted it it to the end of the sentence. So "I am romantic" becomes "because I romantic am".

Let's practise what catapult words do just a couple more times to make sure we haven't forgotten.

How would you say "I am very romantic"?

Ich bin sehr romantisch.
(ikh bin zair roe-marn-tish)

How about "I am not very romantic"?

Ich bin nicht sehr romantisch.
(ikh bin nikht zair roe-marn-tish)

And how would you say "*because* I am not very romantic"?

weil ich nicht sehr romantisch bin
(vile ikh nikht zair roe-marn-tish bin)

What is "drunk" in German?

betrunken
(be-troon-kurn)

And "I am drunk"?

Ich bin betrunken.
(ikh bin be-troon-kurn)

How about "I am very drunk"?

Ich bin sehr betrunken.
(ikh bin zair be-troon-kurn)

And how would you say "because I am very drunk"?

weil ich sehr betrunken bin
(vile ikh zair be-troon-kurn bin)

So, we now know how to use these catapult words, although so far we have only learnt one of them. That will change later in this chapter, however...

First though, let's have another letter swap!

Time to swap some letters!
Letter Swap Number 4

Alright, let's try a fourth letter swap.

This time we'll see how a "**th**" in English can be swapped for a "**d**" in German.

We'll begin by swapping the "**th**" at the beginning of the English word "**th**ing" for a "**d**". This will give us the German word "**D**ing" which, of course, means "thing" in English. Then let's swap the "**th**" in "**th**orn" and so get "**D**orn" in German. And if we do this again with "ba**th**" we get "ba**d**" and with "**th**ick" we get "**d**ick".

So, we have found our equivalent words in German this time by swapping **TH**s for **D**s!

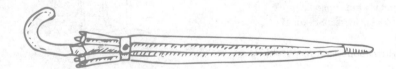

Another excellent letter swap, I think! Of course, sometimes these letters swaps don't work perfectly. An important exception to this most recent letter swap is the word "weather".

"Weather" in German is, unfortunately, not "weader" as letter swap number 4 would lead us to believe. Fortunately, however, it is still very close to the English. "The weather" in German is simply:

das Wetter
(das vet-er)

So how would you say "the weather is good"?

Das Wetter ist gut.
(das vet-er ist goot)

And how about "the weather is not good"?

Das Wetter ist nicht gut.
(das vet-er ist nikht goot)

"So" in German, is, rather wonderfully:

so
(zo)

As you can see, it's spelt in exactly the same way as in English but make sure to pay attention to the pronunciation guidance below it. "So" in German is not pronounced like "so" in English but like the "zo" in the word "zodiac" or the name "Zoe".

So how would you say "the weather is so good"?

Das Wetter ist so gut.
(das vet-er ist zo goot)

How about "the weather is not so good"?

Das Wetter ist nicht so gut.
(das vet-er ist nikht zo goot)

And how would you say "it is not so good"?

Es ist nicht so gut.
(es ist nikht zo goot)

Now, look at the sentence you have just created, "it is not so good" / "es ist nicht so gut". What is the second word in that sentence?

ist
(ist)

So, once again, if we now put a catapult word at the beginning of that sentence, it is this "ist" that will be catapulted to the end of the sentence.

So, how would you say "because it is not so good"?

weil es nicht so gut ist
(vile es nikht zo goot ist)

I'm actually now going to explain how catapult words work in greater detail so that I can introduce more of them to you. But before I do that I'm going to introduce a dreaded grammar term!

A dreaded grammar term...

I'm going to introduce a grammar term now but, before I do, I'm going to make sure that you really understand what it means. If you already know what it means then you can, of course, simply ignore the explanation given in this box. If you don't, however, then please feel free to read through this as many times as you need to.

The grammar term I'm going to introduce is a… *verb*.

If you are reading this book and don't know what a verb is then you will, just by seeing the word written down, have already developed a feeling of grammar dread. Memories of confusion and suffering in language classes at school will be flooding back to you!

Fear not, however, as I'm going to give you an explanation that you will actually understand.

Normally, teachers will tell you that a verb is a *doing* word. Well, if that kind of explanation works for you then *great* but, if not, I'm going to give you a much simpler way to know how to recognise and know what a verb is.

To know if something is a verb, all you need to do is see if you can put "**I**" or "**he**" or "**we**" *directly in front of that word*. If you can and it makes sense then you can feel fairly confident that it's a verb. I'll show you what I mean through some examples:

"I can" – wow, people say "*I can*" all the time (*I* can do it, *I* can see her, *I* can be there at eight). So, since the word "I" can go in front of "can" then "can" must be a verb. Awesome!

"He is" – wow, people say "he is" all the time (he is stupid, he is horrible, he is a bus driver) so "is" must be a verb – we know this because we can put "he" directly in front of it.

"We have" – wow, people say "we have" all the time (we have two cats, we have a dog, we have a son who won't leave home) so "have" must be a verb – we know this because we can put "we" directly in front of it.

Get the idea? Try it yourself. You'll find words that are verbs (like "can", "is", "have" and so on) make sense when you put "I", "he" or "we" etc in front of them, but words that aren't verbs, like "awesome", "dog" or "because" don't make sense at all when you put "I" or "he" or "we" in front of them. Imagine saying "I awesome" or "he dog" or "we because" – they just don't make sense at all. And why? Because those words aren't verbs!

When you say "I dance" or "he drinks" or "we want", however, it becomes very clear that these words are verbs because they do make sense when you put "I" or "he" or "we" in front of them.

So, if you want to know if something is a verb, see if you can put a word like "I" or "he" or "we" directly in front of it!

So, why did I just take the time to introduce what a verb is?

Well, the reason I did this is because the actual rule for how catapult words affect sentences isn't simply that you throw the second word to the end but actually that you throw the *verb* to the end.

And this is in fact what you've been doing so far with the catapult words – I just didn't describe it in that way. For instance, we did it with "it is not so good".

Again, how would you say "it is not so good"?

Es ist nicht so gut.
(es ist nikht zo goot)

And how would you say "because it is not so good"?

weil es nicht so gut ist
(vile es nikht zo goot ist)

So, we've done this before. However, although we thought of it at that time as simply throwing the second word from the original sentence all the way to the end, the technical way of looking at it is that we were actually throwing the verb to the end of the sentence.

And how do we know it's a verb? Well, can we put "I" or "he" or "we" in front of the word that was thrown? The word we threw was "ist" (is) and we can say "he is" so, yes, "is" is clearly a verb.

Now you may wonder, "why is he bothering to teach me this?" I already know which word to throw to the end of the sentence; it's the second word from the original sentence, isn't it?

Well, normally it is, but now that you can identify what a verb is, you have a more foolproof way of being certain which word to catapult: simply throw the verb. In fact, let's throw one now!

What is "the weather" in German?

das Wetter
(das vet-er)

And so how would you say "the weather is so good"?

Das Wetter ist so gut.
(das vet-er ist zo goot)

And how would you say "*because* the weather is so good"? Keeping in mind that "is" is the verb in this sentence.

weil das Wetter so gut ist
(vile das vet-er zo goot ist)

So once again we have thrown the verb to the end of the sentence, which is what catapult words do in German.

How would you say "I am romantic"?

Ich bin romantisch.
(ikh bin roe-marn-tish)

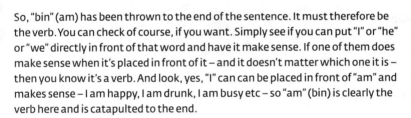

And how would you say "because I am romantic"?

weil ich romantisch bin
(vile ikh roe-marn-tish bin)

So, "bin" (am) has been thrown to the end of the sentence. It must therefore be the verb. You can check of course, if you want. Simply see if you can put "I" or "he" or "we" directly in front of that word and have it make sense. If one of them does make sense when it's placed in front of it – and it doesn't matter which one it is – then you know it's a verb. And look, yes, "I" can can be placed in front of "am" and makes sense – I am happy, I am drunk, I am busy etc – so "am" (bin) is clearly the verb here and is catapulted to the end.

What is "my father"?

mein Vater
(mine far-ter)

And how would you say "my father is romantic"?

Mein Vater ist romantisch.
(mine far-ter ist roe-marn-tish)

And how would you say "because my father is romantic"?

weil mein Vater romantisch ist
(vile mine far-ter roe-marn-tish ist)

So, because we know that it is the verb that gets thrown to the end, we know exactly which word to catapult.

What is "I have" in German?

ich habe
(ikh hah-ber)

And how would you say "I have it"?

Ich habe es.
(ikh hah-ber)

What about "I have seen it"?

Ich habe es gesehen.
(ikh hah-ber es ge-zay-urn)

And "I have done it"?

Ich habe es getan.
(ikh hah-ber es ge-tarn)

What is "we have"?

wir haben
(veer harb-urn)

So how would you say "we have done it"?

Wir haben es getan.
(veer harb-urn es ge-tarn)

How about "we have seen it"?

Wir haben es gesehen.
(veer harb-urn es ge-zay-urn)

"Luck" in German is:

Glück
(g**loo**k)

And to say "we're lucky" in German, you will literally say "we have luck". How would you say that?

Wir haben Glück.
(veer harb-urn glook)

And how would you say "because the weather is so good"?

weil das Wetter so gut ist
(vile das vet-er zo goot ist)

And so how would you say "we're lucky because the weather is so good"?

Wir haben Glück, weil das Wetter so gut ist.
(veer harb-urn glook vile das vet-er zo goot ist)

Okay, that's a lot to absorb in one go. Go away now and take a break before moving on to the second part of the chapter where you'll complete the dialogue given at the beginning of this section. Remember, there's no rush! Berlin wasn't built in a day as they say, or something like that at least...

CHAPTER 6 (2)

We're lucky that the weather's
so good.

We're lucky that the weather's so good.

Person 1:	We're lucky that the weather's so good.
Person 2:	Why?
Person 1:	Because I feel like going to the park.

Time to swap some letters!
Letter Swap Number 5

Alright, fifth letter swap.

This time we'll see how a "**t**" in English can be swapped for an "**s**" or an "**ss**" in German.

We can begin this time by swapping the "**t**" in the English word "wa**t**er" for an "**ss**" in German, which gives us the German word for water: "Wa**ss**er". We can also take "be**tt**er" and, by swapping the **T**s for **S**s, get "be**ss**er". We can also turn "nu**t**" into "Nu**ss**" and "bi**t**" into "bi**ss**". See, it's easy!

So, swap **T**s for **S**s to find the German equivalent!

Okay, we're still building towards this little dialogue. Let's have another letter swap to help us out with it!

This "t" to "s" or "ss" letter swap you've just learnt is very useful in learning German, as it affects a lot of words.

And actually all of the letter swaps become even more useful when you become aware that they don't need to be used in isolation; they can in fact be combined. I'll show you what I mean.

In the last two letter swaps, we learnt both that a "th" in English can be swapped for a "d" in German, and also that a "t" in English can be swapped for an "ss" in German. Knowing this, can you work out what the word for "that" is in German? What do you think it will become once you change the "th" at the beginning to a "d" and the "t" at the end to an "ss"?

dass
(das)

Now again, how would you say "we are lucky" (literally "we have luck")?

Wir haben Glück.
(veer harb-urn glook)

And how would you say "the weather is so good"?

Das Wetter ist so gut.
(das vet-er ist zo goot)

And "because the weather is so good"?

weil das Wetter so gut ist
(vile das vet-er zo goot ist)

And what was "that" in German?

dass
(das)

So, as you now know "dass" (that), I should also let you know that it's a catapult word. So it works just like "weil" (because).

Let's use it!

What is "the weather is so good"?

Das Wetter ist so gut.
(das vet-er ist zo goot)

And how would you say "because the weather is so good"?

weil das Wetter so gut ist
(vile das vet-er zo goot ist)

And so how would you say "...that the weather is so good"?

...dass das Wetter so gut ist
(das das vet-er zo goot ist)

So, just like "weil" (because), "dass" (that) is a catapult word and works in exactly the same way.

Now again, what is "we are lucky" (literally "we have luck")?

Wir haben Glück.
(veer harb-urn glook)

So how would you say "we're lucky that the weather is so good"?

Wir haben Glück, dass das Wetter so gut ist.
(veer harb-urn glook das das vet-er zo goot ist)

What is "the beer"?

das Bier
(das bee-er)

So how would you say "we're lucky that the beer is so good"?

Wir haben Glück, dass das Bier so gut ist.
(veer harb-urn glook das das bee-er zo goot ist)

Now, just on its own, what is "we have"?

wir haben
(veer harb-urn)

And what is "I have"?

ich habe
(ikh hah-ber)

To say "I feel like…" in German, you will literally say "I have lust…" The word for "lust" in German is:

Lust
(loost)

So, how would you say "I feel like…" / "I have lust…"?

Ich habe Lust…
(ikh hah-ber loost)

And how would you say "because I feel like…" / "because I have lust…"?

weil ich Lust habe…
(vile ikh loost hah-ber)

So because "have" is the verb here, it's been thrown after "lust" by the catapult word.

Now, interestingly, "have" and "lust" have an unusual relationship with one another in German: they won't let a catapult word separate them as they're simply too attached to one another! So, although you can catapult "have" onto the other side of "lust" when you're using a catapult word, it won't go any further away than that, *no matter how long you make the sentence.* It will always either be like this:

Ich habe Lust…
(ikh hah-ber loost)

Or, when you use a catapult word, like this:

weil ich Lust habe
(vile ikh loost hah-ber)

But, whatever happens, they stay together – catapult words cannot separate them from one another, they can only move the "habe" to the other side. I'll show you what I mean, just to make this extra clear:

"...to go to the park" or "...going to the park", in German, is literally "in the park to go", which is:

...in den Park zu gehen
(in dain park tsoo gay-urn)

Now again, what is "because I feel like it..." / "because I lust have..."?

weil ich Lust habe...
(vile ikh loost hah-ber)

And again, what was "...to go to the park", (literally "in the park to go")?

...in den Park zu gehen
(in dain park tsoo gay-urn)

And so how would you say "because I feel like going to the park" (keep in mind that "have" and "lust" will stay where they are even though the sentence is about to get longer)?

weil ich Lust habe, in den Park zu gehen
(vile ikh loost hah-ber in dain park tsoo gay-urn)

"To the hotel" in German is literally "in the hotel" which is:

in das Hotel
(in das hotel)

And Germans typically like to shorten the "in das" to "ins". So do that now and tell me, how would you say "to the hotel" in German using this shortened form?

ins Hotel
(ins hotel)

"...to go to the hotel" or "...going to the hotel" would be:

...ins Hotel zu gehen
(ins hotel tsoo gay-urn)

184

Now again, what is "I feel like..."?

Ich habe Lust...
(ikh hah-ber loost)

And what is "because I feel like..."?

weil ich Lust habe...
(vile ikh loost hah-ber)

And what is "to the hotel"?

ins Hotel
(ins hotel)

And what is "...to go to the hotel" or "...going to the hotel"?

...ins Hotel zu gehen
(ins hotel tsoo gay-urn)

So how would you say "because I feel like going to the hotel" (literally "because I have lust in the hotel to go")?

weil ich Lust habe, ins Hotel zu gehen
(vile ikh loost hah-ber ins hotel tsoo gay-urn)

"To the restaurant" is:

ins Restaurant
(ins rest-oh-ron)

So how would you say "because I feel like going to the restaurant"?

weil ich Lust habe, ins Restaurant zu gehen
(vile ikh loost hah-ber ins rest-oh-ron tsoo gay-urn)

And again, how would you say "because I feel like going to the hotel"?

weil ich Lust habe, ins Hotel zu gehen
(vile ikh loost hah-ber ins hotel tsoo gay-urn)

Now, once again, how would you say "the weather is so good"?

Das Wetter ist so gut.
(das vet-er ist zo goot)

And what is "we're lucky"?

Wir haben Glück.
(veer harb-urn glook)

And what is "that"?

dass
(das)

So how would you say "we're lucky that the weather is so good"?

Wir haben Glück, dass das Wetter so gut ist.
(veer harb-urn glook das das vet-er zo goot ist)

"Why?" in German is:

Warum?
(va-room)

Now again, what is "I feel like..."?

Ich habe Lust...
(ikh hah-ber loost)

And what is "because I feel like..."?

weil ich Lust habe...
(vile ikh loost hah-ber)

And again, how would you say "because I feel like going to the restaurant"?

weil ich Lust habe, ins Restaurant zu gehen
(vile ikh loost hah-ber ins rest-oh-ron tsoo gay-urn)

And "because I feel like going to the hotel"?

weil ich Lust habe, ins Hotel zu gehen
(vile ikh loost hah-ber ins hotel tsoo gay-urn)

And what is "to go to the park" (literally "in the park to go")?

in den Park zu gehen
(in dain park tsoo gay-urn)

And so how would you say "because I feel like going to the park"?

weil ich Lust habe, in den Park zu gehen
(vile ikh loost hah-ber in dain park tsoo gay-urn)

And what was the word that meant "why?"

Warum?
(va-room)

Okay, you're now ready to try that dialogue we began the chapter with. Take each sentence slowly and, if you get it wrong, just take another stab at it. It isn't a race and you should just take your time to work it out.

Have a go now:

Person 1:	We're lucky that the weather's so good. Wir haben Glück, dass das Wetter so gut ist. (veer harb-urn glook das das vet-er zo goot ist)
Person 2:	Why? Warum? (va-room)
Person 1:	Because I feel like going to the park. Weil ich Lust habe, in den Park zu gehen. (vile ikh loost hah-ber in dain park tsoo gay-urn)

How did that go? There are some fairly complex aspects of German dealt with in there but as you're probably beginning to notice it is also just a matter of patterns. Learn the patterns and you'll find that you can very quickly begin to communicate in the language, and with a minimum of effort!

Building Blocks 6

Sixth chapter, six new building blocks:

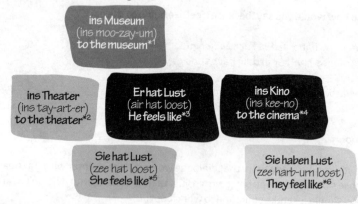

ins Museum
(ins moo-zay-um)
to the museum[1]

ins Theater
(ins tay-art-er)
to the theater[2]

Er hat Lust
(air hat loost)
He feels like[3]

ins Kino
(ins kee-no)
to the cinema[4]

Sie hat Lust
(zee hat loost)
She feels like[5]

Sie haben Lust
(zee harb-urn loost)
They feel like[6]

[1] literally "in the museum"
[2] literally "in the theatre"
[3] literally "he has lust"
[4] literally "in the cinema"
[5] literally "she has lust"
[6] literally "they have lust"

Now, build me some sentences, please!

Er hat Lust
(air hat loost)
He feels like*1

ins Theater
(ins tay-art-er)
to the theater*4

Sie hat Lust
(zee hat loost)
She feels like*2

ins Museum
(ins moo-zay-um)
to the museum*5

zu gehen
(tsoo gay-urn)
go/to go

Sie haben Lust
(zee harb-urn loost)
They feel like*3

ins Kino
(ins kee-no)
to the cinema*6

*1 literally "he has lust"

*2 literally "she has lust"

*3 literally "they have lust"

*4 literally "in the theatre"

*5 literally "in the museum"

*6 literally "in the cinema"

Checklist 6

Checklist number 6, take your time and enjoy it (if you can)!

ich kann (ikh kan)	I can
nicht (nikht)	not
beginnen (baig-in-urn)	begin / to begin
Ich kann nicht beginnen. (ikh kan nikht baig-in-urn)	I cannot begin.
parken (park-urn)	park / to park
bringen (bring-urn)	bring / to bring
campen (camp-urn)	camp / to camp
sie kann (zee kan)	she can

kommen (kom-urn)	come / to come
Sie kann kommen. (zee kan kom-urn)	She can come.
Sie kann nicht kommen. (zee kan nikht kom-urn)	She cannot come.
aber (ah-ber)	but
Sie kann campen aber ich kann nicht kommen. (zee kan camp-urn ah-ber ikh kan nikht kom-urn)	She can camp but I can't come.
heute (hoy-ter)	today
Sie kann heute kommen. (zee kan hoy-ter kom-urn)	She can come today.
hier (hear)	here
Ich kann hier campen. (ikh kan hear camp-urn)	I can camp here.
du kannst (doo kanst)	you can
Du kannst hier parken. (doo kanst hear park-urn)	You can park here.
Kannst du? (kanst doo)	Can you?
heute Nacht (hoy-ter nahkht)	tonight
vorbeikommen (for-by-kom-urn)	come over / to come over / to come by
Kannst du heute Nacht vorbeikommen? (kanst doo hoy-ter nahkht for-by-kom-urn)	Can you come over tonight?
Kann ich? (kan ikh)	Can I?
heute Morgen (hoy-ter mor-gurn)	this morning
Kann ich heute Morgen vorbeikommen? (kan ikh hoy-ter mor-gurn for-by-kom-urn)	Can I come over this morning?
Können wir? (kurn-urn veer)	Can we?
heute Nachmittag (hoy-ter nahkh-mit-arg)	this afternoon
gehen (gay-urn)	go / to go

Können wir heute Nachmittag gehen? (kurn-urn veer hoy-ter nahkh-mit-arg gay-urn)	Can we go this afternoon?
arbeiten (ar-bite-urn)	work / to work
Können wir heute Nachmittag arbeiten? (kurn-urn veer hoy-ter nahkh-mit-arg ar-bite-urn)	Can we work this afternoon?
trinken (trink-urn)	drink / to drink
tanzen (tants-urn)	dance / to dance
ich möchte (ikh murkh-ter)	I would like
sie möchte (zee murkh-ter)	she would like
es (es)	it
tun (toon)	do / to do
jetzt (yetst)	now
ich bin (ikh bin)	I am
betrunken (be-troon-kurn)	drunk
sehr (zair)	very
romantisch (roe-marn-tish)	romantic
beschäftigt (be-shef-tigt)	busy
weil (vile)	because
Kann ich hier trinken? (kan ikh hear trink-urn)	Can I drink here?
Ich möchte hier tanzen. (ikh murkh-ter hear tants-urn)	I would like to dance here.
Ich möchte es nicht. (ikh murkh-ter es nikht)	I wouldn't like it.
Ich möchte es nicht bringen. (ikh murkh-ter es nikht bring-urn)	I wouldn't like to bring it.
Ich möchte es nicht heute tun. (ikh murkh-ter es nikht hoy-ter toon)	I wouldn't like to do it today.
Sie möchte es nicht jetzt bringen. (zee murkh-ter es nikht yetst bring-urn)	She wouldn't like to bring it now.
Ich bin sehr betrunken. (ikh bin zair be-troon-kurn)	I am very drunk.

Ich bin nicht sehr romantisch. (ikh bin nikht zair roe-marn-tish)	I am not very romantic.
Ich bin sehr beschäftigt. (ikh bin zair be-shef-tigt)	I am very busy.
weil ich sehr beschäftigt bin (vile ikh zair be-shef-tigt bin)	because I am very busy
Ich möchte es nicht jetzt tun, weil ich sehr beschäftigt bin. (ikh murkh-ter es nikht yetst toon vile ikh zair be-shef-tigt bin)	I wouldn't like to do it now because I am very busy.
Ich möchte es jetzt bekommen. (ikh murkh-ter es yetzt be-kom-urn)	I would like to get it now.
Sie möchte es später kaufen. (zee murkh-ter es shpay-ter kowf-urn)	She would like to buy it later.
Er möchte es morgen verkaufen. (air murkh-ter es mor-gurn fair-kowf-urn)	He would like to sell it tomorrow.
gut (goot)	good
die Milch (dee milkh)	the milk
Die Milch ist gut. (dee milkh ist goot)	The milk is good.
Ich möchte die Milch trinken. (ikh murkh-ter dee milkh trink-urn)	I would like to drink the milk.
das Bier (das bee-er)	the beer
Das Bier ist gut. (das bee-er ist goot)	The beer is good.
Ich möchte das Bier trinken. (ikh murkh-ter das bee-er trink-urn)	I would like to drink the beer.
der Wein (dair vine)	the wine
Der Wein ist gut. (dair vine ist goot)	The wine is good.
Ich möchte den Wein trinken. (ikh murkh-ter dain vine trink-urn)	I would like to drink the wine.
kaufen (kowf-urn)	buy / to buy
Ich möchte den Wein kaufen. (ikh murkh-ter dain vine kowf-urn)	I would like to buy the wine.
der Tee (dair tay)	the tea

Ich möchte den Tee trinken. (ikh murkh-ter dain tay trink-urn)	I would like to drink the tea.
ich habe (ikh hah-ber)	I have
Ich habe es. (ikh hah-ber es)	I have it.
Ich habe es nicht. (ikh hah-ber es nikht)	I don't have it.
gesehen (ge-zay-urn)	seen
Ich habe es nicht gesehen. (ikh hah-ber es nikht ge-zay-urn)	I haven't seen it / I didn't see it.
weil ich es nicht gesehen habe (vile ikh es nikht ge-zay-urn hah-ber)	because I haven't seen it / because I didn't see it
getan (ge-tarn)	done
Ich habe es getan. (ikh hah-ber es ge-tarn)	I have done it / I did it / I did do it.
der Film (dair film)	the film
Der Film ist nicht sehr gut. (dair film ist nikht zair goot)	The film is not very good.
Ich habe den Film gesehen. (ikh hah-ber den Film ge-zay-urn)	I have seen the film.
das Baby (das bay-bee)	the baby
die Mutter (dee moo-ter)	the mother
der Vater (dair far-ter)	the father
geküsst (ge-koost)	kissed
Ich habe das Baby geküsst. (ikh hah-ber das bay-bee ge-koost)	I have kissed the baby / I kissed the baby / I did kiss the baby.
gekauft (ge-kowft)	bought
Ich habe den Tee gekauft. (ikh hah-ber dain tay ge-kowft)	I have bought the tea / I bought the tea / I did buy the tea.
die Eintrittskarte (dee ine-trits-kart-er)	the ticket
Ich habe die Eintrittskarte gekauft. (ikh hah-ber dee ine-trits-kart-er ge-kowft)	I have bought the ticket / I bought the ticket / I did buy the ticket.
aber (ah-ber)	but

Ich habe die Eintrittskarte gekauft, aber ich habe den Film nicht gesehen. (ikh hah-ber dee ine-trits-kart-er ge-kowft ah-ber ikh hah-ber dain film nikht ge-zay-urn)	I bought the ticket but I didn't see the film.
Ich habe etwas gekauft. (ikh hah-ber et-vas ge-kowft)	I have bought something / I bought something / I did buy something.
Er hat alles verkauft. (air hat al-ez fur-kowft)	He has sold everything / He sold everything / He did sell everything.
Sie hat nichts gesehen. (zee hat nikhts ge-zay-urn)	She has seen nothing / She saw nothing / She did see nothing.
gegeben (ge-gaib-urn)	given
der Taxifahrer (dair taxi-far-er)	the taxi driver (male)
dem Taxifahrer (daim taxi-far-er)	to the taxi driver (male)
Ich habe den Tee dem Taxifahrer gegeben. (ikh hah-ber dain tay daim taxi-far-er ge-gaib-urn)	I have given the tea to the taxi driver / I gave the tea to the taxi driver / I did give the tea to the taxi driver. (male)
das Geld (das gelt)	the money
Ich habe das Geld dem Taxifahrer gegeben. (ikh hah-ber das gelt daim taxi-far-er ge-gaib-urn)	I have given the money to the taxi driver / I gave the money to the taxi driver / I did give the money to the taxi driver. (male)
die Taxifahrerin (dee taxi-far-er-in)	the taxi driver (female)
der Taxifahrerin (dair taxi-far-er-in)	to the taxi driver (female)
Ich habe den Wein der Taxifahrerin gegeben. (ikh hah-ber dain vine dair taxi-far-er-in ge-gaib-urn)	I have given the wine to the taxi driver / I gave the wine to the taxi driver / I did give the wine to the taxi driver. (female)
Ich habe das Geld der Taxifahrerin gegeben. (ikh hah-ber das gelt dair taxi-far-er-in ge-gaib-urn)	I have given the money to the taxi driver / I gave the money to the taxi driver / I did give the money to the taxi driver. (female)
dem Baby (daim bay-bee)	to the baby
Ich habe die Milch dem Baby gegeben. (ikh hah-ber dee milkh daim bay-bee ge-gaib-urn)	I have given the milk to the baby / I gave the milk to the baby / I did give the milk to the baby.

Ich habe den Schlüssel dem Mädchen gegeben. (ikh hah-ber dain shloos-all dem maid-shen ge-gaib-urn)	I have given the key to the girl / I gave the key to the girl / I did give the key to the girl.
Sie haben die Rechnung dem Taxifahrer geschickt. (zee harb-urn dee rekh-nung daim taxi-far-er ge-shikt)	They have sent the bill to the taxi driver / They sent the bill to the taxi driver / They did send the bill to the taxi driver. (male)
Wir haben das Geld der Taxifahrerin geschickt. (veer harb-urn das gelt dair taxi-far-er-in ge-shikt)	We have sent the money to the taxi driver / We sent the money to the taxi driver / We did send the money to the taxi driver. (female)
Es ist gut. (es ist goot)	It is good.
alt (alt)	old
schäbig (shay-big)	shabby
und (oont)	and
mein Auto (mine ow-toe)	my car
Mein Auto ist alt and schäbig. (mine ow-toe ist alt oont shay-big)	My car is old and shabby.
der Vater (dair far-ter)	the father
traurig (trow-rig)	sad
Mein Vater ist traurig. (mine far-ter ist trow-rig)	My father is sad.
das Bier von dem Vater (das bee-er fon daim far-ter)	the father's beer (VM)
die Milch von dem Baby (dee milkh fon daim bay-bee)	the baby's milk (VM)
das Auto von der Mutter (das ow-toe fon dair moo-ter)	the mother's car (VM)
das Bier von meinem Vater (das bee-er fon mine-erm far-ter)	my father's beer (VM)
die Milch von meinem Baby (dee milkh fon mine-erm bay-bee)	my baby's milk (VM)
das Auto von meiner Mutter (das ow-toe fon mine-air moo-ter)	my mother's car (VM)
das Bier meines Vaters (das bee-er mine-es far-ters)	my father's beer (CMFM)

die Milch meines Babys (dee milkh mine-es bay-bees)	my baby's milk (CMFM)
das Auto meiner Mutter (das ow-toe mine-air moo-ter)	my mother's car (CMFM)
Das Auto von meinem Vater ist alt und schäbig. (das ow-toe fon mine-erm far-ter ist alt oont shay-big)	My father's car is old and shabby. (VM)
Das Auto meines Vaters ist alt und schäbig. (das ow-toe mine-es far-ters ist alt oont shay-big)	My father's car is old and shabby. (CMFM)
Das Haus meines Bruders ist brandneu. (das house mine-es broo-ders ist brant-noy)	My brother's house is brand new. (CMFM)
Die Wohnung meiner Schwester ist schmutzig. (dee voe-nung mine-air shves-ter ist shmootzig)	My sister's flat is dirty. (CMFM)
das Wetter (das vet-er)	the weather
so (zo)	so
Das Wetter ist nicht so gut. (das vet-er ist nikht zo goot)	The weather is not so good.
Glück (glook)	luck
Wir haben Glück. (veer harb-urn glook)	We're lucky.
Wir haben Glück, weil das Wetter so gut ist. (veer harb-urn glook vile das vet-er zo goot ist)	We're lucky because the weather is so good.
dass (das)	that
Wir haben Glück, dass das Wetter so gut ist. (veer harb-urn glook das das vet-er zo goot ist)	We're lucky that the weather is so good.
Ich habe Lust... (ikh hah-ber loost)	I feel like...
weil ich Lust habe... (vile ikh loost hah-ber)	because I feel like...
weil ich Lust habe, in den Park zu gehen (vile ikh loost hah-ber in dain park tsoo gay-urn)	because I feel like going to the park

weil ich Lust habe, ins Hotel zu gehen (vile ikh loost hah-ber ins hotel tsoo gay-urn)	because I feel like going to the hotel
weil ich Lust habe, ins Restaurant zu gehen (vile ikh loost hah-ber ins rest-oh-ron tsoo gay-urn)	because I feel like going to the restaurant
Warum? (va-room)	Why?
Er hat Lust, ins Theater zu gehen. (air hat loost ins tay-art-er tsoo gay-urn)	He feels like going to the theatre.
Sie hat Lust, ins Museum zu gehen. (zee hat loost ins moo-zay-um tsoo gay-urn)	She feels like going to the museum.
Sie haben Lust, ins Kino zu gehen. (zee harb-urn loost ins kee-no tsoo gay-urn)	They feel like going to the cinema.

Now enjoy yourself doing it the other way round.

Twice the fun for half the effort... erm... kind of.

I can	ich kann (ikh kan)
not	nicht (nikht)
begin / to begin	beginnen (baig-in-urn)
I cannot begin.	Ich kann nicht beginnen. (ikh kan nikht baig-in-urn)
park / to park	parken (park-urn)
bring / to bring	bringen (bring-urn)
camp / to camp	campen (camp-urn)
she can	sie kann (zee kan)
come / to come	kommen (kom-urn)
She can come.	Sie kann kommen. (zee kan kom-urn)
She cannot come.	Sie kann nicht kommen. (zee kan nikht kom-urn)

but	**aber** (ah-ber)
She can camp but I can't come.	**Sie kann campen aber ich kann nicht kommen.** (zee kan camp-urn ah-ber ikh kan nikht kom-urn)
today	**heute** (hoy-ter)
She can come today.	**Sie kann heute kommen.** (zee kan hoy-ter kom-urn)
here	**hier** (hear)
I can camp here.	**Ich kann hier campen.** (ikh kan hear camp-urn)
you can	**du kannst** (doo kanst)
You can park here.	**Du kannst hier parken.** (doo kanst hear park-urn)
Can you?	**Kannst du?** (kanst doo)
tonight	**heute Nacht** (hoy-ter nahkht)
come over / to come over / to come by	**vorbeikommen** (for-by-kom-urn)
Can you come over tonight?	**Kannst du heute Nacht vorbeikommen?** (kanst doo hoy-ter nahkht for-by-kom-urn)
Can I?	**Kann ich?** (kan ikh)
this morning	**heute Morgen** (hoy-ter mor-gurn)
Can I come over this morning?	**Kann ich heute Morgen vorbeikommen?** (kan ikh hoy-ter mor-gurn for-by-kom-urn)
Can we?	**Können wir?** (kurn-urn veer)
this afternoon	**heute Nachmittag** (hoy-ter nahkh-mit-arg)
go / to go	**gehen** (gay-urn)
Can we go this afternoon?	**Können wir heute Nachmittag gehen?** (kurn-urn veer hoy-ter nahkh-mit-arg gay-urn)
work / to work	**arbeiten** (ar-bite-urn)

Can we work this afternoon?	**Können wir heute Nachmittag arbeiten?** (kurn-urn veer hoy-ter nahkh-mit-arg ar-bite-urn)
drink / to drink	**trinken** (trink-urn)
dance / to dance	**tanzen** (tants-urn)
I would like	**ich möchte** (ikh murkh-ter)
she would like	**sie möchte** (zee murkh-ter)
it	**es** (es)
do / to do	**tun** (toon)
now	**jetzt** (yetst)
I am	**ich bin** (ikh bin)
drunk	**betrunken** (be-troon-kurn)
very	**sehr** (zair)
romantic	**romantisch** (roe-marn-tish)
busy	**beschäftigt** (be-shef-tigt)
because	**weil** (vile)
Can I drink here?	**Kann ich hier trinken?** (kan ikh hear trink-urn)
I would like to dance here.	**Ich möchte hier tanzen.** (ikh murkh-ter hear tants-urn)
I wouldn't like it.	**Ich möchte es nicht.** (ikh murkh-ter es nikht)
I wouldn't like to bring it.	**Ich möchte es nicht bringen.** (ikh murkh-ter es nikht bring-urn)
I wouldn't like to do it today.	**Ich möchte es nicht heute tun.** (ikh murkh-ter es nikht hoy-ter toon)
She wouldn't like to bring it now.	**Sie möchte es nicht jetzt bringen.** (zee murkh-ter es nikht yetst bring-urn)
I am very drunk.	**Ich bin sehr betrunken.** (ikh bin zair be-troon-kurn)
I am not very romantic.	**Ich bin nicht sehr romantisch.** (ikh bin nikht zair roe-marn-tish)

I am very busy.	**Ich bin sehr beschäftigt.** (ikh bin zair be-shef-tigt)
because I am very busy	**weil ich sehr beschäftigt bin** (vile ikh zair be-shef-tigt bin)
I wouldn't like to do it now because I am very busy.	**Ich möchte es nicht jetzt tun, weil ich sehr beschäftigt bin.** (ikh murkh-ter es nikht yetst toon vile ikh zair be-shef-tigt bin)
I would like to get it now.	**Ich möchte es jetzt bekommen.** (ikh murkh-ter es yetzt be-kom-urn)
She would like to buy it later.	**Sie möchte es später kaufen.** (zee murkh-ter es shpay-ter kowf-urn)
He would like to sell it tomorrow.	**Er möchte es morgen verkaufen.** (air murkh-ter es mor-gurn fair-kowf-urn)
good	**gut** (goot)
the milk	**die Milch** (dee milkh)
The milk is good.	**Die Milch ist gut.** (dee milkh ist goot)
I would like to drink the milk.	**Ich möchte die Milch trinken.** (ikh murkh-ter dee milkh trink-urn)
the beer	**das Bier** (das bee-er)
The beer is good.	**Das Bier ist gut.** (das bee-er ist goot)
I would like to drink the beer.	**Ich möchte das Bier trinken.** (ikh murkh-ter das bee-er trink-urn)
the wine	**der Wein** (dair vine)
The wine is good.	**Der Wein ist gut.** (dair vine ist goot)
I would like to drink the wine.	**Ich möchte den Wein trinken.** (ikh murkh-ter dain vine trink-urn)
buy / to buy	**kaufen** (kowf-urn)
I would like to buy the wine.	**Ich möchte den Wein kaufen.** (ikh murkh-ter dain vine kowf-urn)
the tea	**der Tee** (dair tay)
I would like to drink the tea.	**Ich möchte den Tee trinken.** (ikh murkh-ter dain tay trink-urn)
I have	**ich habe** (ikh hah-ber)

I have it.	**Ich habe es.** (ikh hah-ber es)
I don't have it.	**Ich habe es nicht.** (ikh hah-ber es nikht)
seen	**gesehen** (ge-zay-urn)
I haven't seen it / I didn't see it.	**Ich habe es nicht gesehen.** (ikh hah-ber es nikht ge-zay-urn)
because I haven't seen it / because I didn't see it	**weil ich es nicht gesehen habe** (vile ikh es nikht ge-zay-urn hah-ber)
done	**getan** (ge-tarn)
I have done it / I did it / I did do it.	**Ich habe es getan.** (ikh hah-ber es ge-tarn)
the film	**der Film** (dair film)
The film is not very good.	**Der Film ist nicht sehr gut.** (dair film ist nikht zair goot)
I have seen the film.	**Ich habe den Film gesehen.** (ikh hah-ber den Film ge-zay-urn)
the baby	**das Baby** (das bay-bee)
the mother	**die Mutter** (dee moo-ter)
the father	**der Vater** (dair far-ter)
kissed	**geküsst** (ge-koost)
I have kissed the baby / I kissed the baby / I did kiss the baby.	**Ich habe das Baby geküsst.** (ikh hah-ber das bay-bee ge-koost)
bought	**gekauft** (ge-kowft)
I have bought the tea / I bought the tea / I did buy the tea.	**Ich habe den Tee gekauft.** (ikh hah-ber dain tay ge-kowft)
the ticket	**die Eintrittskarte** (dee ine-trits-kart-er)
I have bought the ticket / I bought the ticket / I did buy the ticket.	**Ich habe die Eintrittskarte gekauft.** (ikh hah-ber dee ine-trits-kart-er ge-kowft)
but	**aber** (ah-ber)
I bought the ticket but I didn't see the film.	**Ich habe die Eintrittskarte gekauft, aber ich habe den Film nicht gesehen.** (ikh hah-ber dee ine-trits-kart-er ge-kowft ah-ber ikh hah-ber dain film nikht ge-zay-urn)

I have bought something / I bought something / I did buy something.	Ich habe etwas gekauft. (ikh hah-ber et-vas ge-kowft)
He has sold everything / He sold everything / He did sell everything.	Er hat alles verkauft. (air hat al-ez fur-kowft)
She has seen nothing / She saw nothing / She did see nothing.	Sie hat nichts gesehen. (zee hat nikhts ge-zay-urn)
given	gegeben (ge-gaib-urn)
the taxi driver (male)	der Taxifahrer (dair taxi-far-er)
to the taxi driver (male)	dem Taxifahrer (daim taxi-far-er)
I have given the tea to the taxi driver / I gave the tea to the taxi driver / I did give the tea to the taxi driver. (male)	Ich habe den Tee dem Taxifahrer gegeben. (ikh hah-ber dain tay daim taxi-far-er ge-gaib-urn)
the money	das Geld (das gelt)
I have given the money to the taxi driver / I gave the money to the taxi driver / I did give the money to the taxi driver. (male)	Ich habe das Geld dem Taxifahrer gegeben. (ikh hah-ber das gelt daim taxi-far-er ge-gaib-urn)
the taxi driver (female)	die Taxifahrerin (dee taxi-far-er-in)
to the taxi driver (female)	der Taxifahrerin (dair taxi-far-er-in)
I have given the wine to the taxi driver / I gave the wine to the taxi driver / I did give the wine to the taxi driver. (female)	Ich habe den Wein der Taxifahrerin gegeben. (ikh hah-ber dain vine dair taxi-far-er-in ge-gaib-urn)
I have given the money to the taxi driver / I gave the money to the taxi driver / I did give the money to the taxi driver. (female)	Ich habe das Geld der Taxifahrerin gegeben. (ikh hah-ber das gelt dair taxi-far-er-in ge-gaib-urn)
to the baby	dem Baby (daim bay-bee)
I have given the milk to the baby / I gave the milk to the baby / I did give the milk to the baby.	Ich habe die Milch dem Baby gegeben. (ikh hah-ber dee milkh daim bay-bee ge-gaib-urn)
I have given the key to the girl / I gave the key to the girl / I did give the key to the girl.	Ich habe den Schlüssel dem Mädchen gegeben. (ikh hah-ber dain shloos-all dem maid-shen ge-gaib-urn)

They have sent the bill to the taxi driver / They sent the bill to the taxi driver / They did send the bill to the taxi driver. (male)	Sie haben die Rechnung dem Taxifahrer geschickt. (zee harb-urn dee rekh-nung daim taxi-far-er ge-shikt)
We have sent the money to the taxi driver / We sent the money to the taxi driver / We did send the money to the taxi driver. (female)	Wir haben das Geld der Taxifahrerin geschickt. (veer harb-urn das gelt dair taxi-far-er-in ge-shikt)
It is good.	Es ist gut. (es ist goot)
old	alt (alt)
shabby	schäbig (shay-big)
and	und (oont)
my car	mein Auto (mine ow-toe)
My car is old and shabby.	Mein Auto ist alt and schäbig. (mine ow-toe ist alt oont shay-big)
the father	der Vater (dair far-ter)
sad	traurig (trow-rig)
My father is sad.	Mein Vater ist traurig. (mine far-ter ist trow-rig)
the father's beer (VM)	das Bier von dem Vater (das bee-er fon daim far-ter)
the baby's milk (VM)	die Milch von dem Baby (dee milkh fon daim bay-bee)
the mother's car (VM)	das Auto von der Mutter (das ow-toe fon dair moo-ter)
my father's beer (VM)	das Bier von meinem Vater (das bee-er fon mine-erm far-ter)
my baby's milk (VM)	die Milch von meinem Baby (dee milkh fon mine-erm bay-bee)
my mother's car (VM)	das Auto von meiner Mutter (das ow-toe fon mine-air moo-ter)
my father's beer (CMFM)	das Bier meines Vaters (das bee-er mine-es far-ters)
my baby's milk (CMFM)	die Milch meines Babys (dee milkh mine-es bay-bees)

my mother's car (CMFM)	das Auto meiner Mutter (das ow-toe mine-air moo-ter)
My father's car is old and shabby. (VM)	Das Auto von meinem Vater ist alt und schäbig. (das ow-toe fon mine-erm far-ter ist alt oont shay-big)
My father's car is old and shabby. (CMFM)	Das Auto meines Vaters ist alt und schäbig. (das ow-toe mine-es far-ters ist alt oont shay-big)
My brother's house is brand new. (CMFM)	Das Haus meines Bruders ist brandneu. (das house mine-es broo-ders ist brant-noy)
My sister's flat is dirty. (CMFM)	Die Wohnung meiner Schwester ist schmutzig. (dee voe-nung mine-air shves-ter ist shmootzig)
the weather	das Wetter (das vet-er)
so	so (zo)
The weather is not so good.	Das Wetter ist nicht so gut. (das vet-er ist nikht zo goot)
luck	Glück (glook)
We're lucky.	Wir haben Glück. (veer harb-urn glook)
We're lucky because the weather is so good.	Wir haben Glück, weil das Wetter so gut ist. (veer harb-urn glook vile das vet-er zo goot ist)
that	dass (das)
We're lucky that the weather is so good.	Wir haben Glück, dass das Wetter so gut ist. (veer harb-urn glook das das vet-er zo goot ist)
I feel like…	Ich habe Lust… (ikh hah-ber loost)
because I feel like…	weil ich Lust habe… (vile ikh loost hah-ber)
because I feel like going to the park	weil ich Lust habe, in den Park zu gehen (vile ikh loost hah-ber in dain park tsoo gay-urn)
because I feel like going to the hotel	weil ich Lust habe, ins Hotel zu gehen (vile ikh loost hah-ber ins hotel tsoo gay-urn)

because I feel like going to the restaurant	weil ich Lust habe, ins Restaurant zu gehen (vile ikh loost hah-ber ins rest-oh-ron tsoo gay-urn)
Why?	Warum? (va-room)
He feels like going to the theatre.	Er hat Lust, ins Theater zu gehen. (air hat loost ins tay-art-er tsoo gay-urn)
She feels like going to the museum.	Sie hat Lust, ins Museum zu gehen. (zee hat loost ins moo-zay-um tsoo gay-urn)
They feel like going to the cinema.	Sie haben Lust, ins Kino zu gehen. (zee harb-urn loost ins kee-no tsoo gay-urn)

Wow, Chapter 6 all finished! With each chapter completed, the knowledge you have already gained becomes more secure and your horizons are gradually widened. Have a good break before the next one!

Learn the most common words first

Did you know that the 100 most common words in a language make up roughly 50% of everything you say in any given day, week, month or year?

Or that the 500 most common words make up roughly 90% of everything you say?

Since these extremely common words are so useful, I recommend that, in addition to swapping letters wherever you can, you should also focus as much as possible on those words that are used most often, as these will form the backbone of everything you say.

Of course, you may be wondering, how do I know which words are most common? Well, one way to find this out is to look at word frequency lists that you can find on the internet – boring!

Another way you can use though, is to note down unfamiliar words whenever you see them. Don't bother looking them up right away though. Instead, put a tick next to them every time that you come across them.

Then, at the end of every month, take a look and see which words have the most ticks against them – these are the most common. Feel free now to look these up and write the translation next to all the ticks you've made.

Having written down the translation, don't try to remember it – instead, whenever you encounter those same words again, flick back to your notes and check the meaning.

Doing this each time will guarantee that your focus will always be on the most common words and that you will gradually begin to pick them up!

CHAPTER 7 (1)

Do you think I'm oblivious to
what's going on around me?

Person 1:	We're lucky that the weather's so good.
Person 2:	Why?
Person 1:	Because I feel like going to the park.
Person 2:	Really?
Person 1:	Yes. Why? Don't you feel like going?
Person 2:	Erm, well… I don't have time at the moment.
Person 1:	Really?
Person 2:	Yes, I'm very busy. Very, very busy…
Person 1:	Hey, wait a second… Do you think I'm oblivious to what's going on around me? You have a hangover!
Person 2:	Well, you've got me there!

As you can see, I have massively extended the dialogue from the previous chapter.

You are now going to learn how to complete this conversation, building on what you've learnt already, expanding your range of German expressions as you go.

Now remind me, what is "we're lucky"?

Wir haben Glück.
(veer harb-urn glook)

208

And how would you say "the weather is so good"?

Das Wetter ist so gut.
(das vet-er ist zo goot)

And so how would you say "we're lucky that the weather is so good"?

Wir haben Glück, dass das Wetter so gut ist.
(veer harb-urn glook das das vet-er zo goot ist)

What is "why"?

Warum?
(va-room)

And what is "I feel like..."?

Ich habe Lust…
(ikh hah-ber loost)

And "because I feel like..."?

weil ich Lust habe…
(vile ikh loost hah-ber)

So how would you say "because I feel like going to the restaurant"?

weil ich Lust habe, ins Restaurant zu gehen
(vile ikh loost hah-ber ins rest-oh-ron tsoo gay-urn)

How about "because I feel like going to the hotel"?

weil ich Lust habe, ins Hotel zu gehen
(vile ikh loost hah-ber ins hotel tsoo gay-urn)

And "because I feel like going to the park"?

weil ich Lust habe, in den Park zu gehen
(vile ikh loost hah-ber in dain park tsoo gay-urn)

So, we're now very familiar with how to say "I feel like…" in German: "Ich habe Lust…" (literally, "I have lust…").

Now, to say "I don't feel like…" in German, you will literally say "I have no lust…".

"No lust" in German is:

keine Lust
(kine-er loost)

So how would you say "I don't feel like…" (literally "I have no lust…")?

Ich habe keine Lust…
(ikh hah-ber kine-er loost)

And so how would you say "I don't feel like going to the hotel"?

Ich habe keine Lust, ins Hotel zu gehen.
(ikh hah-ber kine-er loost ins hotel tsoo gay-urn)

And "I don't feel like going to the restaurant"?

Ich habe keine Lust, ins Restaurant zu gehen.
(ikh hah-ber kine-er loost ins rest-oh-ron tsoo gay-urn)

Finally, "I don't feel like going to the park"?

Ich habe keine Lust, in den Park zu gehen.
(ikh hah-ber kine-er loost in dain park tsoo gay-urn)

If you've ever read Shakespeare, you'll know that English speakers used to say "thou hast" to mean "you have"[6]. The modern German for "you have" is really quite similar to "thou hast". It is:

du hast
(doo hast)

So, now that you know how to say "you have", how would you say "you feel like…" (literally "you have lust…")?

Du hast Lust…
(doo hast loost)

Turn this into a question now and ask "do you feel like?" (literally "have you lust?")

Hast du Lust…?
(hast doo loost)

Now try "do you feel like going to the park?" (literally "have you lust in the park to go?")

Hast du Lust, in den Park zu gehen?
(hast doo loost in dain park tsoo gay-urn)

And how about "do you feel like going to the restaurant?"

Hast du Lust, ins Restaurant zu gehen?
(hast doo loost ins rest-oh-ron tsoo gay-urn)

And "do you feel like going to the Hotel?"

Hast du Lust, ins Hotel zu gehen?
(hast doo loost ins hotel tsoo gay-urn)

Now again, what is "I feel like…"?

Ich habe Lust…
(ikh hah-ber loost)

And what is "I don't feel like…"?

Ich habe keine Lust…
(ikh hah-ber kine-er loost)

So how do you think you would you say "you don't feel like…" (literally "you have no lust…")?

Du hast keine Lust…
(doo hast kine-er loost)

Turn this into a question now and ask "don't you feel like…?" (literally "have you no lust…?")

Hast du keine Lust…?
(hast doo kine-er loost)

If you stick "zu gehen" on the end of that sentence, you can ask "don't you feel like going?" Do that now:

Hast du keine Lust zu gehen?
(hast doo kine-er loost tsoo gay-urn)

What is "to camp"?

campen
(camp-urn)

So can you work out how you'd say "don't you feel like camping?"

Hast du keine Lust zu campen?
(hast doo kine-er loost tsoo camp-urn)

What is "to drink"?

trinken
(trink-urn)

So how would you say "don't you feel like drinking?"

Hast du keine Lust zu trinken?
(hast doo kine-er loost tsoo trink-urn)

And how would you say "do you feel like drinking?"

Hast du Lust zu trinken?
(hast doo loost tsoo trink-urn)[7]

---

7 You'll notice that in sentences which talk about "having lust" in German, a "zu" is added just before the end.

So "do you feel like going?" is "hast du Lust zu gehen?" and "do you feel like drinking?" is "hast du Lust zu trinken?"

Don't worry too much if you forget to add the "zu", as you're still likely to be understood but, as you get more practiced with it, you'll find it becomes natural to add this "zu" just before the end of these "lust-having" sentences!

"Yes" in German is:

ja
(yar)

So how would you say "Yes, I feel like drinking"?

Ja, ich habe Lust zu trinken.
(yar ikh hah-ber loost tsoo trink-urn)

How about "yes, I feel like going to the park"?

Ja, ich habe Lust, in den Park zu gehen.
(yar ikh hah-ber loost in dain park tsoo gay-urn)

And "yes, I feel like going to the restaurant"?

Ja, ich habe Lust, ins Restaurant zu gehen.
(yar ikh hah-ber loost ins rest-oh-ron tsoo gay-urn)

Now, just on its own once more, what is "I have"?

ich habe
(ikh hah-ber)

"Time" in German is:

Zeit
(tsite)

So how would you say "I have time"?

Ich habe Zeit.
(ikh hah-ber tsite)

What was "no lust" in German?

keine Lust
(kine-er loost)

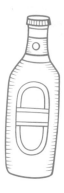

213

So, what would "no time" be?

keine Zeit
(kine-er tsite)

And how would you say "I have no time"?

Ich habe keine Zeit.
(ikh hah-ber kine-er tsite)

And this can be translated as "I have no time" or "I don't have time".

"At the moment" in German is:

im Moment
(im moe-ment)

If you want to say "I don't have time at the moment" in German, you will literally say "I have at the moment no time". How would you say that?

Ich habe im Moment keine Zeit.
(ikh hah-ber im moe-ment kine-er tsite)

"Really" in German is:

wirklich
(verk-likh)

If someone tells you something, such as they don't have time, you can check this, just as you might in English, by simply saying in a questioning tone "really?" Do that now:

Wirklich?
(verk-likh)

Now again, what was "I have time"?

Ich habe Zeit.
(ikh hah-ber tsite)

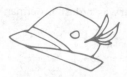

And "I don't have time"?

Ich habe keine Zeit.
(ikh hah-ber kine-er tsite)

And what was "at the moment"?

im Moment
(im moe-ment)

And so how would you say "I don't have time at the moment"?

Ich habe im Moment keine Zeit.
(ikh hah-ber im moe-ment kine-er tsite)

Respond to this, saying "really?"

Wirklich?
(verk-likh)

Now again, how would someone say "I feel like going to the park"?

Ich habe Lust, in den Park zu gehen.
(ikh hah-ber loost in dain park tsoo gay-urn)

Again, respond to this by saying "really?"

Wirklich?
(verk-likh)

And how would the person you were talking to respond back to you, saying "Yes. Why?"

Ja. Warum?
(yar va-room)

Let's try extending this response. This time say, "Yes, why? Don't you feel like going?" (literally "Yes. Why? Have you no lust to go?")

Ja. Warum? Hast du keine Lust zu gehen?
(yar varoom hast doo kine-er loost tsoo gay-urn)

And again, how would you say "I have no time at the moment"?

Ich habe im Moment keine Zeit.
(ikh hah-ber im moe-ment kine-er tsite)

One way to say "Well... or "Erm, well..." in German is:

Na ja...
(nar yar)

So how would you say "Erm, well... I don't have time at the moment"?

Na ja... ich habe im Moment keine Zeit.
(nar yar ikh hah-ber im moe-ment kine-er tsite)

Alright. Feel free to take a break at this point if you need to. Otherwise, you can continue straight on to Part 2. It's up to you, of course, but just make sure not to overdo it in any one session!

CHAPTER 7 (2)

Do you think I'm oblivious to what's going on around me?

On we go with our dialogue then, which, as you will see, is going to teach ever more idiomatic and colloquial language that will help make your German sound more fun, spontaneous, and natural.

What is "I am"?

ich bin
(ikh bin)

And how would you say "I am busy" in German?

Ich bin beschäftigt.
(ikh bin be-shef-tigt)

How about "I am very busy"?

Ich bin sehr beschäftigt.
(ikh bin zair be-shef-tigt)

"Hey..." in German is:

he
(hey)

So how would you say "hey, I'm very busy!"?

He, ich bin sehr beschäftigt!
(hey ikh bin zair be-shef-tigt)

How about "Hey, I'm very hungry!"?

He, ich bin sehr hungrig!
(hey ikh bin zair hoong-grig)

A colloquial way to say "wait a second…" in German is to say something that has a meaning along the lines of "wait once quickly", which is:

Wart' mal schnell…
(vart mal shnel)

Now, remind me, what is "hey" in German?

he
(hey)

So how would you say "Hey, wait a second…"?

He, wart' mal schnell…
(hey vart mal shnel)

This is a good way to show someone you know well that you're somewhat doubtful about what they're saying.

Another way of suggesting that you don't fully believe something you are being told is to say "do you think I'm oblivious to what's going on around me?" The Germans have quite an amusing way of expressing this.

Again, what is "I have"?

ich habe
(ikh hah-ber)

"Tomatoes" in German are:

Tomaten
(tom-art-urn)

So how would you say "I have tomatoes"?

Ich habe Tomaten.
(ikh hah-ber tom-art-urn)

"On the eyes" in German is:

auf den Augen
(*owf dain ow-gurn*)

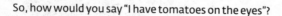

So, how would you say "I have tomatoes on the eyes"?

Ich habe Tomaten auf den Augen.
(ikh hah-ber tom-art-urn owf dain ow-gurn)

In German, this would mean that you were oblivious to what was going to around you.

So, how would you say "because I'm oblivious to what's going on" (literally "because I tomatoes on the eyes have")?

weil ich Tomaten auf den Augen habe
(vile ich tom-art-urn owf dain ow-gurn hah-ber)

You'll notice, of course, that the catapult word "weil" (because) has as usual thrown the verb, on this occasion "habe" (have), to the end of the sentence.

Let's do exactly the same thing again with the catapult word "dass" (that).

So how would you say "…that I'm oblivious to what's going on" (literally "that I tomatoes on the eyes have")?

…dass ich Tomaten auf den Augen habe
(das ikh tom-art-urn owf dain ow-gurn hah-ber)

"Do you think?" in German is more or less "think'st thou?" (again, it's all there in Shakespeare[8]) which in German is:

Denkst du?
(*denkst doo*)

---

8 "O think'st thou we shall ever meet again?" (Romeo and Juliet, Act 3 Scene 5)

Now again what was "...that I'm oblivious to what's going on" (literally "that I tomatoes on the eyes have")?

...dass ich Tomaten auf den Augen habe
(das ikh tom-art-urn owf dain ow-gurn hah-ber)

And what was "do you think?" / "think'st thou?"

Denkst du?
(denkst doo)

So how would you say "do you think that I'm oblivious to what's going on?"

Denkst du, dass ich Tomaten auf den Augen habe?
(denkst doo das ikh tom-art-urn owf dain ow-gurn hah-ber)

Now again, what was "well..." / "erm, well..."

Na ja...
(nar yar)

If you want to say "gotcha!" in German, you will literally say "caught!" which is:

Erwischt!
(air-visht)

Now you can just say this on its own or you can include it as part of a sentence. For example, what is "you have"?

du hast
(doo hast)

So how would you say "you have caught"?

du hast erwischt
(doo hast air-visht)

"me" in German is:

mich
(mikh)

So how would you say "you've got me!" / "you've caught me!" (literally "you have me caught!")?

Du hast mich erwischt!
(*doo hast* mikh air-visht)

If you want to make this sound more natural you can add the German word for "there" into the sentence to make it into "you've got me there".

"There" in German is:

da
(dar)

So, say now, "you've got me there!", bearing in mind that Germans will literally say "there have you me caught!"

Da hast du mich erwischt!
(dar hast *doo* mikh air-visht)

Again, what is "well…" / "erm, well…"

Na ja…
(nar yar)

So how would you say "Well, you've got me there!"?

Na ja, da hast du mich erwischt!
(nar yar dar hast *doo* mikh air-visht)

You'll find that words such as "na ja" (erm, well..."), "he" (hey) or even "da" (there) can really give much more feeling to a German sentence and make it sound far more natural and like everyday language. Getting used to the examples you're learning here will help you begin to develop a feel for when and where to insert them into your German sentences.

Another word frequently used to do this is "yes". What is "yes" in German?

ja
(yar)

If you add "ja" (yes) into a sentence it can also help add some feeling or nuance of meaning. I'll show you what I mean.

"A tomcat" in German is:

ein Kater
(ine[9] kar-ter)

What is "you have"?

du hast
(doo hast)

Now, I want you, in a moment, to say "you have a tomcat" but I also want you to be aware that a tomcat is masculine and so, as it is the thing on the receiving end of the sentence (it is the thing being had) "ein" will change to "einen", just as "der" turned to "den" in earlier chapters when something was being done to that masculine thing.

So, bearing in mind that "ein" will become "einen", how would you say "you have a tomcat"?

Du hast einen Kater.
(doo hast ine-urn kar-ter)

---

9   "Ein" is pronounced like the "ine" in the English words "mine" or "pine".

Now, saying that someone has a tomcat is actually the way that you say they have a hangover in German. Perhaps Germans feel having a hangover is like having a tomcat running around inside their heads. Who knows!

Anyway, give me that sentence again, how would you say in German "you have a hangover"?

Du hast einen Kater.
(*doo hast ine-urn kar-ter*)

Now, that's fine as a sentence, but if you want to add a bit of feeling into it to more or less express the feeling "Oh yeah, I know what you've been up to, you have a hangover!" you can simply stick "ja" (yes) into the middle of it and this will help add that sort of flavour and feeling to it. So, do that now, say "You have yes a hangover!"

Du hast ja einen Kater!
(*doo hast yar ine-urn kar-ter*)

Good. You'll slowly get used to doing this as your German becomes more sophisticated and as you are exposed to more of the language.

Now, let's start to get ready for that dialogue again.

So again, what is "we are lucky"?

Wir haben Glück.
(*veer harb-urn glook*)

And how would you say "the weather is so good"?

Das Wetter ist so gut.
(*das vet-er ist zo goot*)

And "we're lucky that the weather is so good"?

Wir haben Glück, dass das Wetter so gut ist.
(*veer harb-urn glook das das vet-er zo goot ist*)

And what is "I feel like..."?

Ich habe Lust…
(ikh hah-ber loost)

And so how would you say "I feel like going to the restaurant"?

Ich habe Lust, ins Restaurant zu gehen.
(ikh hah-ber loost ins rest-oh-ron tsoo gay-urn)

And "I feel like going to the park"?

Ich habe Lust, in den Park zu gehen.
(ikh hah-ber loost in dain park tsoo gay-urn)

And "I don't feel like going to the park"?

Ich habe keine Lust, in den Park zu gehen.
(ikh hah-ber kine-er loost in dain park tsoo gay-urn)

What is "you feel like..."?

Du hast Lust…
(doo hast loost)

So how would you say "you feel like going to the park"?

Du hast Lust, in den Park zu gehen.
(doo hast loost in dain park tsoo gay-urn)

And what about "you don't feel like going to the park"?

Du hast keine Lust, in den Park zu gehen.
(doo hast kine-er loost in dain park tsoo gay-urn)

And how would you say "don't you feel like going to the park?" (literally "have you no lust in the park to go?")

Hast du keine Lust, in den Park zu gehen?
(hast doo kine-er loost in dain park tsoo gay-urn)

And how about simply "don't you feel like going?" (literally "have you no lust to go?")

Hast du keine Lust zu gehen?
(hast doo kine-er loost tsoo gay-urn)

What is "really"?

wirklich
(verk-likh)

And what is "why?"

Warum?
(va-room)

And what is "at the moment"?

im Moment
(im moe-ment)

And how would you say "I don't have time"?

Ich habe keine Zeit.
(ikh hah-ber kine-er tsite)

And "I don't have time at the moment"?

Ich habe im Moment keine Zeit.
(ikh hah-ber im moe-ment kine-er tsite)

What is "well…" / "erm, well…"?

Na ja…
(nar yar)

And so how would you say "Erm, well... I don't have time at the moment"?

Na ja… ich habe im Moment keine Zeit.
(nar yar ikh hah-ber im moe-ment kine-er tsite)

What is "busy"?

beschäftigt
(be-shef-tigt)

So how would you say "very, very busy"?

sehr, sehr beschäftigt
(zair zair be-shef-tigt)

And how would you say "I am busy. Very, very busy"?

Ich bin beschäftigt. Sehr, sehr beschäftigt.
(ikh bin be-shef-tigt zair zair be-shef-tigt)

What is "hey"?

he
(hey)

And what was "wait a second..." (more or less literally "wait once quickly")?

Wart' mal schnell…
(hey vart mal shnel)

So how would you say "hey, wait a second…"?

He, wart' mal schnell…
(hey vart mal shnel)

What was "do you think?"?

denkst du?
(denkst doo)

And how would you say "I have tomatoes on the eyes"?

Ich habe Tomaten auf den Augen.
(ikh hah-ber tom-art-urn owf dain ow-gurn)

How about "...that I have tomatoes on the eyes"?

...dass ich Tomaten auf den Augen habe
(das ikh tom-art-urn owf dain ow-gurn hah-ber)

And so how would you say "do you think that I'm oblivious to what's going on?"
(literally "do you think that I tomatoes on the eyes have?")

Denkst du, dass ich Tomaten auf den Augen habe?
(denkst doo das ikh tom-art-urn owf dain ow-gurn hah-ber)

Now, put these together and say "Hey, wait a second. Do you think I'm oblivious
to what's going on?"

He, wart' mal schnell... Denkst du, dass ich Tomaten auf den Augen habe?
(hey vart mal shnel denkst doo das ikh tom-art-urn owf dain ow-gurn hah-ber)

And again, what was the word for "hangover" (literally "tomcat")?

Kater
(kar-ter)

So how would you say "you've got a hangover!" (literally "you have yes a tomcat!")?

Du hast ja einen Kater!
(doo hast yar ine-urn kar-ter)

Now let's add all of this together and say "Hey, wait a second... Do you think I'm
oblivious to what's going on? You've got a hangover!"

He, wart' mal schnell... Denkst du, dass ich Tomaten auf den Augen habe?
Du hast ja einen Kater!
(hey vart mal shnel denkst doo das ikh tom-art-urn owf dain ow-gurn hah-ber
doo hast yar ine-urn kar-ter)

What is the word for "caught"?

erwischt
(air-visht)

And do you remember what "me" was?

mich
(mikh)

And so how would you say "you've caught me" / "you've got me" (literally "you have me caught")?

Du hast mich erwischt!
(doo hast mikh air-visht)

What is the word for "there"?

da
(dar)

So, how would you say "you've got me there!" / "there have you me caught!"?

Da hast du mich erwischt!
(dar hast doo mikh air-visht)

And, putting this all together to make it even more colloquial, how would you say "Well, you've got me there!" (literally "Well, there have you me caught!")?

Na ja, da hast du mich erwischt!
(nar yar dar hast doo mikh air-visht)

Alright. I think it's time for you to have a go at the long dialogue from the beginning of the chapter for which I've been preparing you.

Try going through it, slowly the first couple of times and then, once you feel confident enough, see if you can get to the point where you can construct the entire dialogue without needing to pause. It will take a fair amount of practice but, every time you go through it, it will greatly benefit your German.

Are you ready then? Take your time and off you go with the final dialogue:

We're lucky that the weather's so good.
Wir haben Glück, dass das Wetter so gut ist.
(veer harb-urn glook das das vet-er zo goot ist)

Why?
Warum?
(va-room)

Because I feel like going to the park.
Weil ich Lust habe, in den Park zu gehen.
(vile ikh loost hah-ber in dain park tsoo gay-urn)

Really?
Wirklich?
(verk-likh)

Yes. Why? Don't you feel like going?
Ja. Warum? Hast du keine Lust zu gehen?
(yar varoom hast doo kine-er loost tsoo gay-urn)

Erm, well… I don't have time at the moment.
Na ja… ich habe im Moment keine Zeit.
(nar yar ikh hah-ber im moe-ment kine-er tsite)

Really?
Wirklich?
(verk-likh)

Yes, I'm busy. Very, very busy…
Ja, ich bin beschäftigt. Sehr, sehr beschäftigt…
(yar ikh bin be-shef-tigt zair zair be-shef-tigt)

Hey, wait a second... Do you think I'm oblivious to what's going on? You've got a hangover!

He, wart' mal schnell... Denkst du, dass ich Tomaten auf den Augen habe? Du hast ja einen Kater!

(hey vart mal shnel denkst doo das ikh tom-art-urn owf dain ow-gurn hah-ber doo hast yar ine-urn kar-ter)

Well, you've got me there!

Na ja, da hast du mich erwischt!

(nar yar dar hast doo mikh air-visht)

Checklist 7

Well, that's it! You've just finished your final chapter, which makes this your final checklist. Unlike the ones that came before it, however, you are not finished with this checklist until you can go the whole way through it without making a single mistake.

This doesn't mean that making mistakes when you go through it is a bad thing. It's just that I want you to return to it multiple times until going through the list becomes so easy that you can do it without making a single error.

When you can, it means you have really learnt what I wanted to teach you in these pages.

Now, get to it!

ich kann (ikh kan)	I can
nicht (nikht)	not
beginnen (baig-in-urn)	begin / to begin
Ich kann nicht beginnen. (ikh kan nikht baig-in-urn)	I cannot begin.
parken (park-urn)	park / to park
bringen (bring-urn)	bring / to bring
campen (camp-urn)	camp / to camp
sie kann (zee kan)	she can

kommen (kom-urn)	come / to come
Sie kann kommen. (zee kan kom-urn)	She can come.
Sie kann nicht kommen. (zee kan nikht kom-urn)	She cannot come.
aber (ah-ber)	but
Sie kann campen aber ich kann nicht kommen. (zee kan camp-urn ah-ber ikh kan nikht kom-urn)	She can camp but I can't come.
heute (hoy-ter)	today
Sie kann heute kommen. (zee kan hoy-ter kom-urn)	She can come today.
hier (hear)	here
Ich kann hier campen. (ikh kan hear camp-urn)	I can camp here.
du kannst (doo kanst)	you can
Du kannst hier parken. (doo kanst hear park-urn)	You can park here.
Kannst du? (kanst doo)	Can you?
heute Nacht (hoy-ter nahkht)	tonight
vorbeikommen (for-by-kom-urn)	come over / to come over / to come by
Kannst du heute Nacht vorbeikommen? (kanst doo hoy-ter nahkht for-by-kom-urn)	Can you come over tonight?
Kann ich? (kan ikh)	Can I?
heute Morgen (hoy-ter mor-gurn)	this morning
Kann ich heute Morgen vorbeikommen? (kan ikh hoy-ter mor-gurn for-by-kom-urn)	Can I come over this morning?
Können wir? (kurn-urn veer)	Can we?
heute Nachmittag (hoy-ter nahkh-mit-arg)	this afternoon
gehen (gay-urn)	go / to go

Können wir heute Nachmittag gehen? (kurn-urn veer hoy-ter nahkh-mit-arg gay-urn)	Can we go this afternoon?
arbeiten (ar-bite-urn)	work / to work
Können wir heute Nachmittag arbeiten? (kurn-urn veer hoy-ter nahkh-mit-arg ar-bite-urn)	Can we work this afternoon?
trinken (trink-urn)	drink / to drink
tanzen (tants-urn)	dance / to dance
ich möchte (ikh murkh-ter)	I would like
sie möchte (zee murkh-ter)	she would like
es (es)	it
tun (toon)	do / to do
jetzt (yetst)	now
ich bin (ikh bin)	I am
betrunken (be-troon-kurn)	drunk
sehr (zair)	very
romantisch (roe-marn-tish)	romantic
beschäftigt (be-shef-tigt)	busy
weil (vile)	because
Kann ich hier trinken? (kan ikh hear trink-urn)	Can I drink here?
Ich möchte hier tanzen. (ikh murkh-ter hear tants-urn)	I would like to dance here.
Ich möchte es nicht. (ikh murkh-ter es nikht)	I wouldn't like it.
Ich möchte es nicht bringen. (ikh murkh-ter es nikht bring-urn)	I wouldn't like to bring it.
Ich möchte es nicht heute tun. (ikh murkh-ter es nikht hoy-ter toon)	I wouldn't like to do it today.
Sie möchte es nicht jetzt bringen. (zee murkh-ter es nikht yetst bring-urn)	She wouldn't like to bring it now.

Ich bin sehr betrunken. (ikh bin zair be-troon-kurn)	I am very drunk.
Ich bin nicht sehr romantisch. (ikh bin nikht zair roe-marn-tish)	I am not very romantic.
Ich bin sehr beschäftigt. (ikh bin zair be-shef-tigt)	I am very busy.
weil ich sehr beschäftigt bin (vile ikh zair be-shef-tigt bin)	because I am very busy
Ich möchte es nicht jetzt tun, weil ich sehr beschäftigt bin. (ikh murkh-ter es nikht yetst toon vile ikh zair be-shef-tigt bin)	I wouldn't like to do it now because I am very busy.
Ich möchte es jetzt bekommen. (ikh murkh-ter es yetzt be-kom-urn)	I would like to get it now.
Sie möchte es später kaufen. (zee murkh-ter es shpay-ter kowf-urn)	She would like to buy it later.
Er möchte es morgen verkaufen. (air murkh-ter es mor-gurn fair-kowf-urn)	He would like to sell it tomorrow.
gut (goot)	good
die Milch (dee milkh)	the milk
Die Milch ist gut. (dee milkh ist goot)	The milk is good.
Ich möchte die Milch trinken. (ikh murkh-ter dee milkh trink-urn)	I would like to drink the milk.
das Bier (das bee-er)	the beer
Das Bier ist gut. (das bee-er ist goot)	The beer is good.
Ich möchte das Bier trinken. (ikh murkh-ter das bee-er trink-urn)	I would like to drink the beer.
der Wein (dair vine)	the wine
Der Wein ist gut. (dair vine ist goot)	The wine is good.
Ich möchte den Wein trinken. (ikh murkh-ter dain vine trink-urn)	I would like to drink the wine.
kaufen (kowf-urn)	buy / to buy
Ich möchte den Wein kaufen. (ikh murkh-ter dain vine kowf-urn)	I would like to buy the wine.

der Tee (dair tay)	the tea
Ich möchte den Tee trinken. (ikh murkh-ter dain tay trink-urn)	I would like to drink the tea.
ich habe (ikh hah-ber)	I have
Ich habe es. (ikh hah-ber es)	I have it.
Ich habe es nicht. (ikh hah-ber es nikht)	I don't have it.
gesehen (ge-zay-urn)	seen
Ich habe es nicht gesehen. (ikh hah-ber es nikht ge-zay-urn)	I haven't seen it / I didn't see it.
weil ich es nicht gesehen habe (vile ikh es nikht ge-zay-urn hah-ber)	because I haven't seen it / because I didn't see it
getan (ge-tarn)	done
Ich habe es getan. (ikh hah-ber es ge-tarn)	I have done it / I did it / I did do it.
der Film (dair film)	the film
Der Film ist nicht sehr gut. (dair film ist nikht zair goot)	The film is not very good.
Ich habe den Film gesehen. (ikh hah-ber den Film ge-zay-urn)	I have seen the film.
das Baby (das bay-bee)	the baby
die Mutter (dee moo-ter)	the mother
der Vater (dair far-ter)	the father
geküsst (ge-koost)	kissed
Ich habe das Baby geküsst. (ikh hah-ber das bay-bee ge-koost)	I have kissed the baby / I kissed the baby / I did kiss the baby.
gekauft (ge-kowft)	bought
Ich habe den Tee gekauft. (ikh hah-ber dain tay ge-kowft)	I have bought the tea / I bought the tea / I did buy the tea.
die Eintrittskarte (dee ine-trits-kart-er)	the ticket
Ich habe die Eintrittskarte gekauft. (ikh hah-ber dee ine-trits-kart-er ge-kowft)	I have bought the ticket / I bought the ticket / I did buy the ticket.

aber (ah-ber)	but
Ich habe die Eintrittskarte gekauft, aber ich habe den Film nicht gesehen. (ikh hah-ber dee ine-trits-kart-er ge-kowft ah-ber ikh hah-ber dain film nikht ge-zay-urn)	I bought the ticket but I didn't see the film.
Ich habe etwas gekauft. (ikh hah-ber et-vas ge-kowft)	I have bought something / I bought something / I did buy something.
Er hat alles verkauft. (air hat al-ez fur-kowft)	He has sold everything / He sold everything / He did sell everything.
Sie hat nichts gesehen. (zee hat nikhts ge-zay-urn)	She has seen nothing / She saw nothing / She did see nothing.
gegeben (ge-gaib-urn)	given
der Taxifahrer (dair taxi-far-er)	the taxi driver (male)
dem Taxifahrer (daim taxi-far-er)	to the taxi driver (male)
Ich habe den Tee dem Taxifahrer gegeben. (ikh hah-ber dain tay daim taxi-far-er ge-gaib-urn)	I have given the tea to the taxi driver / I gave the tea to the taxi driver / I did give the tea to the taxi driver. (male)
das Geld (das gelt)	the money
Ich habe das Geld dem Taxifahrer gegeben. (ikh hah-ber das gelt daim taxi-far-er ge-gaib-urn)	I have given the money to the taxi driver / I gave the money to the taxi driver / I did give the money to the taxi driver. (male)
die Taxifahrerin (dee taxi-far-er-in)	the taxi driver (female)
der Taxifahrerin (dair taxi-far-er-in)	to the taxi driver (female)
Ich habe den Wein der Taxifahrerin gegeben. (ikh hah-ber dain vine dair taxi-far-er-in ge-gaib-urn)	I have given the wine to the taxi driver / I gave the wine to the taxi driver / I did give the wine to the taxi driver. (female)
Ich habe das Geld der Taxifahrerin gegeben. (ikh hah-ber das gelt dair taxi-far-er-in ge-gaib-urn)	I have given the money to the taxi driver / I gave the money to the taxi driver / I did give the money to the taxi driver. (female)
dem Baby (daim bay-bee)	to the baby

Ich habe die Milch dem Baby gegeben. (ikh hah-ber dee milkh daim bay-bee ge-gaib-urn)	I have given the milk to the baby / I gave the milk to the baby / I did give the milk to the baby.
Ich habe den Schlüssel dem Mädchen gegeben. (ikh hah-ber dain shloos-all dem maid-shen ge-gaib-urn)	I have given the key to the girl / I gave the key to the girl / I did give the key to the girl.
Sie haben die Rechnung dem Taxifahrer geschickt. (zee harb-urn dee rekh-nung daim taxi-far-er ge-shikt)	They have sent the bill to the taxi driver / They sent the bill to the taxi driver / They did send the bill to the taxi driver. (male)
Wir haben das Geld der Taxifahrerin geschickt. (veer harb-urn das gelt dair taxi-far-er-in ge-shikt)	We have sent the money to the taxi driver / We sent the money to the taxi driver / We did send the money to the taxi driver. (female)
Es ist gut. (es ist goot)	It is good.
alt (alt)	old
schäbig (shay-big)	shabby
und (oont)	and
mein Auto (mine ow-toe)	my car
Mein Auto ist alt and schäbig. (mine ow-toe ist alt oont shay-big)	My car is old and shabby.
der Vater (dair far-ter)	the father
traurig (trow-rig)	sad
Mein Vater ist traurig. (mine far-ter ist trow-rig)	My father is sad.
das Bier von dem Vater (das bee-er fon daim far-ter)	the father's beer (VM)
die Milch von dem Baby (dee milkh fon daim bay-bee)	the baby's milk (VM)
das Auto von der Mutter (das ow-toe fon dair moo-ter)	the mother's car (VM)
das Bier von meinem Vater (das bee-er fon mine-erm far-ter)	my father's beer (VM)
die Milch von meinem Baby (dee milkh fon mine-erm bay-bee)	my baby's milk (VM)

das Auto von meiner Mutter (das ow-toe fon mine-air moo-ter)	my mother's car (VM)
das Bier meines Vaters (das bee-er mine-es far-ters)	my father's beer (CMFM)
die Milch meines Babys (dee milkh mine-es bay-bees)	my baby's milk (CMFM)
das Auto meiner Mutter (das ow-toe mine-air moo-ter)	my mother's car (CMFM)
Das Auto von meinem Vater ist alt und schäbig. (das ow-toe fon mine-erm far-ter ist alt oont shay-big)	My father's car is old and shabby. (VM)
Das Auto meines Vaters ist alt und schäbig. (das ow-toe mine-es far-ters ist alt oont shay-big)	My father's car is old and shabby. (CMFM)
Das Haus meines Bruders ist brandneu. (das house mine-es broo-ders ist brant-noy)	My brother's house is brand new. (CMFM)
Die Wohnung meiner Schwester ist schmutzig. (dee voe-nung mine-air shves-ter ist shmootzig)	My sister's flat is dirty. (CMFM)
das Wetter (das vet-er)	the weather
so (zo)	so
Das Wetter ist nicht so gut. (das vet-er ist nikht zo goot)	The weather is not so good.
Glück (glook)	luck
Wir haben Glück. (veer harb-urn glook)	We're lucky.
Wir haben Glück, weil das Wetter so gut ist. (veer harb-urn glook vile das vet-er zo goot ist)	We're lucky because the weather is so good.
dass (das)	that
Wir haben Glück, dass das Wetter so gut ist. (veer harb-urn glook das das vet-er zo goot ist)	We're lucky that the weather is so good.
Ich habe Lust… (ikh hah-ber loost)	I feel like…

weil ich Lust habe... (vile ikh loost hah-ber)	because I feel like...
weil ich Lust habe, in den Park zu gehen (vile ikh loost hah-ber in dain park tsoo gay-urn)	because I feel like going to the park
weil ich Lust habe, ins Hotel zu gehen (vile ikh loost hah-ber ins hotel tsoo gay-urn)	because I feel like going to the hotel
weil ich Lust habe, ins Restaurant zu gehen (vile ikh loost hah-ber ins rest-oh-ron tsoo gay-urn)	because I feel like going to the restaurant
Warum? (va-room)	Why?
Er hat Lust, ins Theater zu gehen. (air hat loost ins tay-art-er tsoo gay-urn)	He feels like going to the theatre.
Sie hat Lust, ins Museum zu gehen. (zee hat loost ins moo-zay-um tsoo gay-urn)	She feels like going to the museum.
Sie haben Lust, ins Kino zu gehen. (zee harb-urn loost ins kee-no tsoo gay-urn)	They feel like going to the cinema.
Wirklich? (verk-likh)	Really?
Ja. (yar)	Yes.
du hast (doo hast)	you have
Ja. Warum? Hast du keine Lust zu gehen? (yar varoom hast doo kine-er loost tsoo gay-urn)	Yes. Why? Don't you feel like going?
Na ja... (nar yar)	Well... / Erm, well...
im Moment (im moe-ment)	at the moment
Na ja... ich habe im Moment keine Zeit. (nar yar ikh hah-ber im moe-ment kine-er tsite)	Erm, well... I don't have time at the moment.
Ja, ich bin beschäftigt. Sehr, sehr beschäftigt... (yar ikh bin be-shef-tigt zair zair be-shef-tigt)	Yes, I'm busy. Very, very busy...

he (hey)	hey
Wart' mal schnell… (vart mal shnel)	Wait a second…
Denkst du? (denkst doo)	Do you think?
ein Kater (ine kar-ter)	a hangover
Du hast ja einen Kater! (doo hast yar ine-urn kar-ter)	You have a hangover!
He, wart' mal schnell… Denkst du, dass ich Tomaten auf den Augen habe? Du hast ja einen Kater! (hey vart mal shnel denkst doo das ikh tom-art-urn owf dain ow-gurn hah-ber doo hast yar ine-urn kar-ter)	Hey, wait a second… Do you think I'm oblivious to what's going on? You've got a hangover!
erwischt (air-visht)	caught
da (dar)	there
Na ja, da hast du mich erwischt! (nar yar dar hast doo mikh air-visht)	Well, you've got me there!

Having worked your way through the German-to-English list above without making any mistakes, you will now want to get to the point where you can also work through English-to-German list below without making any mistakes. You should feel free to do this over several days or even weeks if you feel you need to. Just take your time and work at it until constructing the sentences and recalling the words become second nature to you.

I can	ich kann (ikh kan)
not	nicht (nikht)
begin / to begin	beginnen (baig-in-urn)
I cannot begin.	Ich kann nicht beginnen. (ikh kan nikht baig-in-urn)
park / to park	parken (park-urn)
bring / to bring	bringen (bring-urn)
camp / to camp	campen (camp-urn)
she can	sie kann (zee kan)
come / to come	kommen (kom-urn)

She can come.	Sie kann kommen. (zee kan kom-urn)
She cannot come.	Sie kann nicht kommen. (zee kan nikht kom-urn)
but	aber (ah-ber)
She can camp but I can't come.	Sie kann campen aber ich kann nicht kommen. (zee kan camp-urn ah-ber ikh kan nikht kom-urn)
today	heute (hoy-ter)
She can come today.	Sie kann heute kommen. (zee kan hoy-ter kom-urn)
here	hier (hear)
I can camp here.	Ich kann hier campen. (ikh kan hear camp-urn)
you can	du kannst (doo kanst)
You can park here.	Du kannst hier parken. (doo kanst hear park-urn)
Can you?	Kannst du? (kanst doo)
tonight	heute Nacht (hoy-ter nahkht)
come over / to come over / to come by	vorbeikommen (for-by-kom-urn)
Can you come over tonight?	Kannst du heute Nacht vorbeikommen? (kanst doo hoy-ter nahkht for-by-kom-urn)
Can I?	Kann ich? (kan ikh)
this morning	heute Morgen (hoy-ter mor-gurn)
Can I come over this morning?	Kann ich heute Morgen vorbeikommen? (kan ikh hoy-ter mor-gurn for-by-kom-urn)
Can we?	Können wir? (kurn-urn veer)
this afternoon	heute Nachmittag (hoy-ter nahkh-mit-arg)
go / to go	gehen (gay-urn)
Can we go this afternoon?	Können wir heute Nachmittag gehen? (kurn-urn veer hoy-ter nahkh-mit-arg gay-urn)

work / to work	arbeiten (ar-bite-urn)
Can we work this afternoon?	Können wir heute Nachmittag arbeiten? (kurn-urn veer hoy-ter nahkh-mit-arg ar-bite-urn)
drink / to drink	trinken (trink-urn)
dance / to dance	tanzen (tants-urn)
I would like	ich möchte (ikh murkh-ter)
she would like	sie möchte (zee murkh-ter)
it	es (es)
do / to do	tun (toon)
now	jetzt (yetst)
I am	ich bin (ikh bin)
drunk	betrunken (be-troon-kurn)
very	sehr (zair)
romantic	romantisch (roe-marn-tish)
busy	beschäftigt (be-shef-tigt)
because	weil (vile)
Can I drink here?	Kann ich hier trinken? (kan ikh hear trink-urn)
I would like to dance here.	Ich möchte hier tanzen. (ikh murkh-ter hear tants-urn)
I wouldn't like it.	Ich möchte es nicht. (ikh murkh-ter es nikht)
I wouldn't like to bring it.	Ich möchte es nicht bringen. (ikh murkh-ter es nikht bring-urn)
I wouldn't like to do it today.	Ich möchte es nicht heute tun. (ikh murkh-ter es nikht hoy-ter toon)
She wouldn't like to bring it now.	Sie möchte es nicht jetzt bringen. (zee murkh-ter es nikht yetst bring-urn)
I am very drunk.	Ich bin sehr betrunken. (ikh bin zair be-troon-kurn)
I am not very romantic.	Ich bin nicht sehr romantisch. (ikh bin nikht zair roe-marn-tish)

I am very busy.	Ich bin sehr beschäftigt. (ikh bin zair be-shef-tigt)
because I am very busy	weil ich sehr beschäftigt bin (vile ikh zair be-shef-tigt bin)
I wouldn't like to do it now because I am very busy.	Ich möchte es nicht jetzt tun, weil ich sehr beschäftigt bin. (ikh murkh-ter es nikht yetst toon vile ikh zair be-shef-tigt bin)
I would like to get it now.	Ich möchte es jetzt bekommen. (ikh murkh-ter es yetzt be-kom-urn)
She would like to buy it later.	Sie möchte es später kaufen. (zee murkh-ter es shpay-ter kowf-urn)
He would like to sell it tomorrow.	Er möchte es morgen verkaufen. (air murkh-ter es mor-gurn fair-kowf-urn)
good	gut (goot)
the milk	die Milch (dee milkh)
The milk is good.	Die Milch ist gut. (dee milkh ist goot)
I would like to drink the milk.	Ich möchte die Milch trinken. (ikh murkh-ter dee milkh trink-urn)
the beer	das Bier (das bee-er)
The beer is good.	Das Bier ist gut. (das bee-er ist goot)
I would like to drink the beer.	Ich möchte das Bier trinken. (ikh murkh-ter das bee-er trink-urn)
the wine	der Wein (dair vine)
The wine is good.	Der Wein ist gut. (dair vine ist goot)
I would like to drink the wine.	Ich möchte den Wein trinken. (ikh murkh-ter dain vine trink-urn)
buy / to buy	kaufen (kowf-urn)
I would like to buy the wine.	Ich möchte den Wein kaufen. (ikh murkh-ter dain vine kowf-urn)
the tea	der Tee (dair tay)
I would like to drink the tea.	Ich möchte den Tee trinken. (ikh murkh-ter dain tay trink-urn)

I have	ich habe (ikh hah-ber)
I have it.	Ich habe es. (ikh hah-ber es)
I don't have it.	Ich habe es nicht. (ikh hah-ber es nikht)
seen	gesehen (ge-zay-urn)
I haven't seen it / I didn't see it.	Ich habe es nicht gesehen. (ikh hah-ber es nikht ge-zay-urn)
because I haven't seen it / because I didn't see it	weil ich es nicht gesehen habe (vile ikh es nikht ge-zay-urn hah-ber)
done	getan (ge-tarn)
I have done it / I did it / I did do it.	Ich habe es getan. (ikh hah-ber es ge-tarn)
the film	der Film (dair film)
The film is not very good.	Der Film ist nicht sehr gut. (dair film ist nikht zair goot)
I have seen the film.	Ich habe den Film gesehen. (ikh hah-ber den Film ge-zay-urn)
the baby	das Baby (das bay-bee)
the mother	die Mutter (dee moo-ter)
the father	der Vater (dair far-ter)
kissed	geküsst (ge-koost)
I have kissed the baby / I kissed the baby / I did kiss the baby.	Ich habe das Baby geküsst. (ikh hah-ber das bay-bee ge-koost)
bought	gekauft (ge-kowft)
I have bought the tea / I bought the tea / I did buy the tea.	Ich habe den Tee gekauft. (ikh hah-ber dain tay ge-kowft)
the ticket	die Eintrittskarte (dee ine-trits-kart-er)
I have bought the ticket / I bought the ticket / I did buy the ticket.	Ich habe die Eintrittskarte gekauft. (ikh hah-ber dee ine-trits-kart-er ge-kowft)
but	aber (ah-ber)

I bought the ticket but I didn't see the film.	Ich habe die Eintrittskarte gekauft, aber ich habe den Film nicht gesehen. (ikh hah-ber dee ine-trits-kart-er ge-kowft ah-ber ikh hah-ber dain film nikht ge-zay-urn)
I have bought something / I bought something / I did buy something.	Ich habe etwas gekauft. (ikh hah-ber et-vas ge-kowft)
He has sold everything / He sold everything / He did sell everything.	Er hat alles verkauft. (air hat al-ez fur-kowft)
She has seen nothing / She saw nothing / She did see nothing.	Sie hat nichts gesehen. (zee hat nikhts ge-zay-urn)
given	gegeben (ge-gaib-urn)
the taxi driver (male)	der Taxifahrer (dair taxi-far-er)
to the taxi driver (male)	dem Taxifahrer (daim taxi-far-er)
I have given the tea to the taxi driver / I gave the tea to the taxi driver / I did give the tea to the taxi driver. (male)	Ich habe den Tee dem Taxifahrer gegeben. (ikh hah-ber dain tay daim taxi-far-er ge-gaib-urn)
the money	das Geld (das gelt)
I have given the money to the taxi driver / I gave the money to the taxi driver / I did give the money to the taxi driver. (male)	Ich habe das Geld dem Taxifahrer gegeben. (ikh hah-ber das gelt daim taxi-far-er ge-gaib-urn)
the taxi driver (female)	die Taxifahrerin (dee taxi-far-er-in)
to the taxi driver (female)	der Taxifahrerin (dair taxi-far-er-in)
I have given the wine to the taxi driver / I gave the wine to the taxi driver / I did give the wine to the taxi driver. (female)	Ich habe den Wein der Taxifahrerin gegeben. (ikh hah-ber dain vine dair taxi-far-er-in ge-gaib-urn)
I have given the money to the taxi driver / I gave the money to the taxi driver / I did give the money to the taxi driver. (female)	Ich habe das Geld der Taxifahrerin gegeben. (ikh hah-ber das gelt dair taxi-far-er-in ge-gaib-urn)
to the baby	dem Baby (daim bay-bee)
I have given the milk to the baby / I gave the milk to the baby / I did give the milk to the baby.	Ich habe die Milch dem Baby gegeben. (ikh hah-ber dee milkh daim bay-bee ge-gaib-urn)

I have given the key to the girl / I gave the key to the girl / I did give the key to the girl.	Ich habe den Schlüssel dem Mädchen gegeben. (ikh hah-ber dain shloos-all dem maid-shen ge-gaib-urn)
They have sent the bill to the taxi driver / They sent the bill to the taxi driver / They did send the bill to the taxi driver. (male)	Sie haben die Rechnung dem Taxifahrer geschickt. (zee harb-urn dee rekh-nung daim taxi-far-er ge-shikt)
We have sent the money to the taxi driver / We sent the money to the taxi driver / We did send the money to the taxi driver. (female)	Wir haben das Geld der Taxifahrerin geschickt. (veer harb-urn das gelt dair taxi-far-er-in ge-shikt)
It is good.	Es ist gut. (es ist goot)
old	alt (alt)
shabby	schäbig (shay-big)
and	und (oont)
my car	mein Auto (mine ow-toe)
My car is old and shabby.	Mein Auto ist alt and schäbig. (mine ow-toe ist alt oont shay-big)
the father	der Vater (dair far-ter)
sad	traurig (trow-rig)
My father is sad.	Mein Vater ist traurig. (mine far-ter ist trow-rig)
the father's beer (VM)	das Bier von dem Vater (das bee-er fon daim far-ter)
the baby's milk (VM)	die Milch von dem Baby (dee milkh fon daim bay-bee)
the mother's car (VM)	das Auto von der Mutter (das ow-toe fon dair moo-ter)
my father's beer (VM)	das Bier von meinem Vater (das bee-er fon mine-erm far-ter)
my baby's milk (VM)	die Milch von meinem Baby (dee milkh fon mine-erm bay-bee)
my mother's car (VM)	das Auto von meiner Mutter (das ow-toe fon mine-air moo-ter)

my father's beer (CMFM)	das Bier meines Vaters (das bee-er mine-es far-ters)
my baby's milk (CMFM)	die Milch meines Babys (dee milkh mine-es bay-bees)
my mother's car (CMFM)	das Auto meiner Mutter (das ow-toe mine-air moo-ter)
My father's car is old and shabby. (VM)	Das Auto von meinem Vater ist alt und schäbig. (das ow-toe fon mine-erm far-ter ist alt oont shay-big)
My father's car is old and shabby. (CMFM)	Das Auto meines Vaters ist alt und schäbig. (das ow-toe mine-es far-ters ist alt oont shay-big)
My brother's house is brand new. (CMFM)	Das Haus meines Bruders ist brandneu. (das house mine-es broo-ders ist brant-noy)
My sister's flat is dirty. (CMFM)	Die Wohnung meiner Schwester ist schmutzig. (dee voe-nung mine-air shves-ter ist shmootzig)
the weather	das Wetter (das vet-er)
so	so (zo)
The weather is not so good.	Das Wetter ist nicht so gut. (das vet-er ist nikht zo goot)
luck	Glück (glook)
We're lucky.	Wir haben Glück. (veer harb-urn glook)
We're lucky because the weather is so good.	Wir haben Glück, weil das Wetter so gut ist. (veer harb-urn glook vile das vet-er zo goot ist)
that	dass (das)
We're lucky that the weather is so good.	Wir haben Glück, dass das Wetter so gut ist. (veer harb-urn glook das das vet-er zo goot ist)
I feel like...	Ich habe Lust... (ikh hah-ber loost)
because I feel like...	weil ich Lust habe... (vile ikh loost hah-ber)

because I feel like going to the park	weil ich Lust habe, in den Park zu gehen (vile ikh loost hah-ber in dain park tsoo gay-urn)
because I feel like going to the hotel	weil ich Lust habe, ins Hotel zu gehen (vile ikh loost hah-ber ins hotel tsoo gay-urn)
because I feel like going to the restaurant	weil ich Lust habe, ins Restaurant zu gehen (vile ikh loost hah-ber ins rest-oh-ron tsoo gay-urn)
Why?	Warum? (va-room)
He feels like going to the theatre.	Er hat Lust, ins Theater zu gehen. (air hat loost ins tay-art-er tsoo gay-urn)
She feels like going to the museum.	Sie hat Lust, ins Museum zu gehen. (zee hat loost ins moo-zay-um tsoo gay-urn)
They feel like going to the cinema.	Sie haben Lust, ins Kino zu gehen. (zee harb-urn loost ins kee-no tsoo gay-urn)
Really?	Wirklich? (verk-likh)
Yes.	Ja. (yar)
you have	du hast (doo hast)
Yes. Why? Don't you feel like going?	Ja. Warum? Hast du keine Lust zu gehen? (yar varoom hast doo kine-er loost tsoo gay-urn)
Well… / Erm, well…	Na ja… (nar yar)
at the moment	im Moment (im moe-ment)
Erm, well… I don't have time at the moment.	Na ja… ich habe im Moment keine Zeit. (nar yar ikh hah-ber im moe-ment kine-er tsite)
Yes, I'm busy. Very, very busy…	Ja, ich bin beschäftigt. Sehr, sehr beschäftigt… (yar ikh bin be-shef-tigt zair zair be-shef-tigt)
hey	he (hey)
Wait a second…	Wart' mal schnell… (vart mal shnel)

Do you think?	**Denkst du?** (denkst doo)
a hangover	**ein Kater** (ine kar-ter)
Hey, wait a second... Do you think I'm oblivious to what's going on? You've got a hangover!	**He, wart' mal schnell... Denkst du, dass ich Tomaten auf den Augen habe? Du hast ja einen Kater!** (hey vart mal shnel denkst doo das ikh tom-art-urn owf dain ow-gurn hah-ber doo hast yar ine-urn kar-ter)
caught	**erwischt** (air-visht)
there	**da** (dar)
Well, you've got me there!	**Na ja, da hast du mich erwischt!** (nar yar dar hast doo mikh air-visht)

If you've got through this without making any mistakes then you're ready to read the final Between Chapters Tip and then the last section of the book, which tells you what to do next.

Well done for getting this far! Well done indeed...

The Great Letter Swap!

Since the very beginning of the book, I've been giving you examples of how you can rapidly build up your German vocabulary by swapping letters. Really though, what I've shown you so far has only been the tip of that enormous iceberg I mentioned in the Introduction.

Below, I'm going to show you a number of additional letter swaps that will help you to create or interperet many more German words.

Once you've had a read through them, I recommend that you try coming up with a few more examples for each and then check in a dictionary to see whether you've successfully created the corresponding German word.

Have fun!

An English letter ...	is often a ... in German	Examples
d	t	hard = hart old = alt cold = kalt to drink = trinken
th	d	thing = Ding thorn = Dorn thou = du to thank = danken
k	ch	milk = Milch book = Buch to make = machen to break = brechen
y	g	day = Tag to say = sagen to lay = legen to fly = fliegen
gh	ch	night = Nacht sight = Sicht light = Licht daughter = Tochter

An English letter ...	is often a ... in German	Examples
y (at the end of a describing word)	ig	hungry = hungrig hasty = hastig frosty = frostig sandy = sandig
p (at or near the beginning of a word)	pf	plaster = Pflaster pan = Pfanne[10] pepper = Pfeffer path = Pfad
p (in the middle or at the end of a word)	f	sharp = scharf ship = Schiff to help = helfen ripe = reif
v (in the middle or at the end of a word)	b	to have = haben to live = leben to give = geben seven = sieben
t (in the middle or at the end of a word)	s or ss	that = dass what? = was? water = Wasser better = besser

Remember, try to come up with some examples of your own and then check in a dictionary to see if they work. I'll give you a few suggestions you can begin with if you'd like: silver, God, deep, and week. Take a guess as to what they will become in German, based on the letter swaps described above, and then look them up to see how close the reality comes to the theory.

This is a really good way to build vocabulary quickly and easily – so take advantage of it!

---

10   You may have noticed while reading this book that certain words that are not capitalised in English are written with a capital letter in German.

This is because, in English, we write the names of people and places with capital letters but in German they go further. Not only do they write the names of people and places in capitals but also the names of things. So, anything that you can give a name to – a table, a hat, a car, a pan – will have a capital letter in German.

This is certainly not something for you to worry about but I just wanted to let you know in case you were wondering why capitals are often present in the German translation even when they are not there in the equivalent English sentence. This is why...

Between Chapters Tip!

What to do next

Well, here you are at the end of the final chapter. You have worked hard and yet a different journey now lies ahead of you!

The questions you should be asking, of course, are: "what is that journey exactly?" and "where do I go from here?" – essentially, "what should I do next?"

Where do you go first?

Well, that will depend to some degree on what you already knew when you began working through this book.

If you *have* found this book useful then I would recommend moving on to the audio course that I have produced entitled "Learn German with Paul Noble". It uses the same method as this book except that you listen to it rather than read it. It will help to develop your understanding of how to structure German sentences and how to use German tenses, while at the same time gently expanding your vocabulary in the language as well as teaching you plenty of tricks that will allow you to make rapid progress.

And after that?

Once you have completed the audio course, I then recommend that you use what I have at different times called "The Frasier Method", "The Game of Thrones Method", "The Buffy the Vampire Slayer Method" and "The Friends Method" – but the name isn't too important.

What is important is how the method works, which is like this...

Once you have gained a functional vocabulary and understanding of structures and tenses (from having used both this book and my audio course), I recommend that you then purchase an *English* language television series – a long one. It should ideally have something like 50 episodes or more (100 is even better). And it should be something that you have watched previously.

This might seem an odd way to learn German but it's not. Trust me. It is in fact a very easy and enjoyable way to develop your ability in the language. Now listen well because I'm going to explain to you exactly how this method works.

Almost all major successful long-running English language TV series will be available with a German dub. Typically, the version you can buy locally will have the ability to switch the language to German, if not you can go to eBay or Amazon Germany and order the German dubbed version from there.

Now, what you're going to do with the series you've chosen is to watch it in German, one episode at a time, whenever it's convenient for you to do so. And, when you watch it, you're not only going to watch it dubbed into German but you're also going to put on the *German* subtitles. If you use the English subtitles, you will spend your whole time reading them and will learn nothing.

Now while you watch the German dub of the series you've chosen, I want you to keep a pen and notepad handy and, when you hear a word you're not familiar with, I want you to write it down. Do this with the first twenty words you don't recognise. Once you've written those twenty down, don't bother writing any more for the rest of the episode. Instead, all I want you you to do is to put a tick beside each of those words every time you hear them during the rest of that same episode.

When the episode is finished, take a look at how many ticks each word has. Any word with more than three ticks by the side of it is something you need to learn. So, look it up in a dictionary and then write the English word beside it in your notepad. Once you have a translation for each, use the checklist technique utilised in this book to go through them until you can remember roughly what each word means. Then let yourself forget about them.

The following day, repeat this whole process again during the next episode. Something you'll begin to notice very quickly, however, is that those words that came up a lot in the first episode will also come up a lot in the second. This is because, on the one hand, any words that came up a lot the first day are likely to be quite important words anyway and, on the other, because you're watching a TV series, the same themes are typically repeated in different episodes. So, if you like *Game of Thrones*, you're going to very quickly learn the words for things such as "castle", "horse" and "wench". If you like *Friends* then you're going to very quickly learn the words for things like "coffee shop", "girl friend" and "break up".

And it's precisely because these same themes and the same language come up again and again that watching a long series becomes much more valuable than simply watching something like German films, for example. Were you to watch German films instead, you would quickly find that each film would almost certainly have a different theme and therefore the vocabulary would not repeat itself so much. When you watch a TV series, however, because you're looking up the most important vocabulary, and because it's repeated in the series again and again and again, you really do end up remembering it. It becomes extremely familiar to you.

Now, you may say to this "okay, fair enough, but why does it have to be an English language series dubbed into German rather than simply a German one? And why should it be something I've seen before in English, why not something totally new?" Well, the reason for this is simple: you will learn far more, far more quickly doing it this way. And why? Well, because if you decide to watch a German TV series, instead of an English one, you will immediately encounter unfamiliar cultural issues – the way people live, where they do their shopping, what they cook – much of this will be different. This therefore means that, if you watch a German TV series, you will not only be trying to figure out what something means linguistically but also, very frequently, what something means culturally. It will simply present another set of barriers to understanding, which is why it's best to begin with something familiar.

This leads us on to why it should be a series that you've already watched in English before. For the exact same reasons given a moment ago, you should try to choose a TV series you've watched before because you will already be familiar with the context of the story. This will make it far easier to grasp what is being said, to catch words, to get the jokes and to increase your understanding more rapidly. Often, you will find that you can actually guess what a particular word means because you are already familiar with the context and this will make it far easier to pick up that word in German.

So, once you're finished with this book and my audio course (you will need to have done both to be ready to use this "Game of Thrones Method"), go and watch a TV series and keep a pen and notepad handy and use it in exactly the way I've describe above.

If you do this, both you and your German will soar!

Good Luck! - Viel Glück!

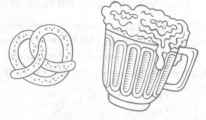

PRONUNCIATION GUIDE

A guide to pronunciation is provided under *every* word and sentence in this book. However, in case you're still struggling with any of the trickier German words and sounds, I wanted to let you know about an additional resource that is also available to you.

Forvo

One wonderful resource that should help you with the pronunciation of more or less any German word is Forvo.

Forvo is a free service, which also requires no membership and no logins, where thousands of native speaker volunteers have recorded themselves saying various words from their languages.

So, if you're not sure whether you've got the pronunciation of a word quite right and it's worrying you, then simply go to forvo.com and type in that word. Frequently, you will find that the word has been recorded by several different people and so you can listen to multiple examples of the word until you feel confident that you know how to pronounce it.

So, if in doubt, go to forvo.com and have a listen!

**Newport Community
Learning & Libraries**

BELOW

26·1·18

BETTWS